Treating Youth
with **DSM-IV** Disorders
The Role of Social Skill Instruction

Also from the Boys Town Press

Changing Children's Behavior by Changing the People,
    Places, and Activities in Their Lives
No Room for Bullies
Tools for Teaching Social Skills in School
Practical Tools for Foster Parents
Time to Enrich Before and After School Activity Kits
Who's Raising Your Child?
Teaching Social Skills to Youth, 2nd Edition
Basic Social Skills for Youth
Angry Kids, Frustrated Parents
Dangerous Kids
Rebuilding Children's Lives
Building Skills in High-Risk Families
Skills for Families, Skills for Life
Good Night, Sweet Dreams, I Love You: Now Get into Bed and Go to Sleep!
Working with Aggressive Youth
Effective Skills for Child-Care Workers
Caring for Youth in Shelters
Parenting to Build Character in Your Teen
Common Sense Parenting®
Common Sense Parenting® of Toddlers and Preschoolers
Common Sense Parenting Learn-at-Home Video Kit
The Well-Managed Classroom
Safe and Effective Secondary Schools
Unmasking Sexual Con Games
Boundaries: A Guide for Teens
Dealing with Your Kids' 7 Biggest Troubles
Parents and Kids Talking about School Violence
Getting Along with Others
A Good Friend
Who's in the Mirror?
What's Right for Me?

www.boystownpress.org
For a free Boys Town Press catalog, call 1-800-282-6657

**The Girls and Boys Town National Hotline is a 24-hour crisis line
for parents and children with any problem. 1-800-448-3000**

Treating Youth
with DSM-IV Disorders

The Role of Social Skill Instruction

A proven teaching approach that enhances the treatment provided
to troubled youth by mental health professionals and others

BY MICHAEL STERBA, M.H.D. AND TOM DOWD, M.A.

BOYS TOWN PRESS

Boys Town, Nebraska

Treating Youth with DSM-IV Disorders

Published by The Boys Town Press
Father Flanagan's Boys' Home
Boys Town, Nebraska 68010

The Boys Town Press is the publishing division of Girls and Boys Town, the original Father Flanagan's Boys' Home.

Publisher's Cataloging-in-Publication

(Provided by Quality Books, Inc.)

Sterba, Michael.
Treating youth with DSM-IV disorders : the role of social skill instruction / by Michael Sterba, Tom Dowd. – 1 st ed.
p. cm.
Includes index.
ISBN: 1-889322-29-6

1. Behavior therapy for teenagers. 2. Behavior therapy for children. 3. Social skills in children—Study and teaching.
4. Diagnostic and statistical manual of mental disorders.
I. Dowd, Tom. II. Title.

RJ505.B4S84 1998   371.94
                                 QBI98-737

10 9 8 7 6 5

Acknowledgments

This book would not have been possible without the commitment and ongoing efforts of many people. We would like to thank the following people for their contributions to this book: Father Val J. Peter, Executive Director of Boys Town; Thomas Criste, Director of Behavioral Health Services, and Executive Director of the Boys Town Residential Treatment Center; Katherine Dinges, Program Director of the Boys Town Residential Treatment Center; Jeff Tierney, Director of Boys Town Staff Training; Tom Waite, Site Director, Boys Town of Nevada; Wendy Partridge-Waite, Coordinator of Residential Family Services, Boys Town of Nevada.

A special thanks to the American Psychiatric Association for allowing us to use selected portions of the *Diagnostic and Statistical Manual of Mental Health Disorders (DSM-IV)* in this book. The cooperation of the American Psychiatric Association is greatly appreciated.

Table of Contents

Introduction

'Slow Learner' Kevin

Kevin, an 11-year-old boy, is described by his parents and teachers as a child whose "motor is always running." It's been that way since Kevin entered kindergarten at age five. In the classroom, it is difficult for Kevin to pay or sustain attention; he doesn't concentrate on details and, as a result, makes careless mistakes in his schoolwork. Kevin's teachers frequently reprimand him for interrupting others, not waiting his turn, and constantly talking to other classmates during study time, even when the students are given time to quietly do something they like. Often, Kevin is out of his chair, asking the teacher if he can get a drink or go to the bathroom; when he does remain at his desk, he fidgets and squirms in his seat. He regularly loses his homework and textbooks or forgets to bring them home, and when he does remember, his parents report "it's like pulling teeth" to get him to sit down for any length of time to complete his studies. As a result, his grades are failing, even though his teachers say he's capable of doing the work.

At home, it is more of the same. Kevin forgets to do chores and has trouble sitting through dinner or a family activity. His father thinks Kevin is "lazy" and "irresponsible,"

1

and that he would do better in school and at home if he just "applied himself and tried harder." Lately, Kevin and his father have had heated arguments over Kevin's failing schoolwork and his forgetfulness regarding his chores. Kevin's relationships with his parents, brother and sisters, teachers, and friends are becoming strained, causing Kevin further frustration and resulting in more frequent temper outbursts.

'Unmanageable' Dwayne

Over the past year, Dwayne's temper has gotten worse. He frequently "loses his cool" when his mother asks him to help out at home or do his chores. At these times, Dwayne argues and often gets into shouting matches with his mother; he curses, openly tests her authority, and is verbally aggressive. Dwayne's mother describes her 12-year-old son as stubborn and unwilling to compromise or negotiate with her. She says, "He wants it his way or no way." Many times, Dwayne refuses his mother's requests by simply ignoring her, and purposely breaks the rules she makes. She tries to discipline Dwayne by "grounding" him or not letting him watch TV or talk on the phone, but he doesn't accept the consequences. He won't take responsibility for his behavior and constantly makes up stories and lies, or blames others for his misdeeds.

These same behaviors are becoming more and more prevalent at school. His teachers are frustrated by his constant challenges to their authority, rules, and consequences. Dwayne is spending more time in the office for his defiance, and his schoolwork is suffering. When he is in class, his teachers report, he deliberately annoys other students, and is spiteful and vindictive toward students and teachers whom he believes "have done him wrong."

Recently, he was kicked out of the local mall by a security officer after the officer questioned Dwayne and a friend about a shoplifting incident that neither boy was involved in. During the questioning, Dwayne got mad and threatened the security guard. Dwayne doesn't have many friends anymore, and his mother considers the ones he does have to be "troublemakers." His mother, at the end her rope, placed Dwayne in a residential group home program.

'Down in the Dumps' Jamie

Twice during the past year, 13-year-old Jamie tried to commit suicide and was placed in an inpatient psychiatric program by her parents. The first attempt was 10 months ago when Jamie overdosed on aspirin; recently, she cut her wrists. She says she tried to hurt herself because she is "no good" and "didn't care any more." During the same period, Jamie has been "down in the dumps" several times. These cycles often last a few weeks.

During these stretches, her parents report that Jamie has no energy and constantly seems tired and fatigued; they often find her tearful and crying. It's almost impossible to get her to go to school, where she usually is a good student and is active in school activities and sports. Once an "A" and "B" student, her grades have dropped dramatically and she is currently failing most of her classes. Jamie's teachers are concerned; they report she has difficulty concentrating, is easily distracted, and is unable to make simple decisions like what subject to write on for an English paper. Most surprisingly, Jamie doesn't have any interest in going to play practice. She usually loves this activity and has been in many plays since she was very young. Three months ago, when she wasn't in one of her "down cycles," she earned a major role in the school play; now she wants to quit. Jamie says she is no good and would only "screw it up."

At meals, Jamie just picks at her favorite foods; she is a slim girl so the weight loss is noticeable. Often, she stays up watching TV into the early morning hours. Jamie says she wakes up in the middle of the night and can't get back to sleep. During the day, she is irritable and spends most of her time alone in her room. Her friends call and ask her to go out but she says she is too tired. Her parents are afraid she might succeed in hurting herself and "want the old Jamie back."

DSM-IV Diagnoses

It is obvious that the youngsters described in these three examples lack certain social skills that would enable them to better cope with everyday life. But for these kids, and many others like them, skill deficiency is only one element of a much bigger problem – a mental health disorder. Kevin's behaviors and related symptoms point to Attention-Deficit/Hyper-activity Disorder; the temper outbursts and aggression displayed by Dwayne could be signs of Oppositional Defiant Disorder; and Jamie's attempts to hurt herself indicate Major Depressive Disorder.

These types of diagnoses are possible because of the advancements and improvements made over the last 45 years in the *Diagnostic and Statistical Manual of Mental Health Disorders* (*DSM-IV*), the world's standard tool for evaluating and diagnosing mental health disorders in children, adolescents, and adults. This progress in classifying and identifying mental health disorders has lead to instruction and training for mental health professionals that is more intensely focused on how to effectively treat youth who have specific mental health disorder diagnoses. This, in turn, has lead to more appropriate and accurate treatment for youth.

Helping parents and caregivers improve the treatment they provide is the goal of this book. As we said earlier, a lack of certain social skills contributes to, and often exacerbates, an existing mental health disorder. That is why Boys Town believes that social skill instruction – teaching youth alternative positive behaviors that they can use to replace current inappro-priate behaviors – should be a key ingredient of any Treatment Plan.

Through years of experience working with thousands of children and adolescents with behavioral and mental disorders, Boys Town's research has proven that social skill instruction is extremely effective in helping youth overcome their problems. By showing how this social skill instruction approach can be applied to the treatment of *DSM-IV* disorders, we hope to provide a valuable guide for parents and caregivers that will help them effectively and successfully treat youth in their care. (Caregivers can include youth-care workers, Family-Teachers, Consultants, shelter workers and administrators, family interventionists, staff working in psychiatric settings, teachers, school counselors, therapists, social workers, psychiatrists, physicians, psychologists, clinicians, and other health and mental health professionals.)

What's in This Book

There are six parts to this book. A history of the *DSM-IV* is outlined in the first chapter along with an introduction to the importance of other assessment and evaluation tools. Also, there is an explanation of the multiaxial assessment system – detailed in the *DSM-IV* – that can help mental health professionals during the evaluation process. A discussion of ethnicity and cultural awareness regarding *DSM-IV* mental health disorder diagnoses and social skill instruction follows in the second chapter.

The third chapter discusses the Boys Town Teaching Model, the Boys Town Social Skill Curriculum, the concept of social skill instruction, and the importance and effectiveness of such teaching in the treatment of *DSM-IV* disorders.

Chapter 4 offers a series of charts that contain 43 *DSM-IV* diagnoses that are common for children and adolescents, the diagnostic criteria as they appear in the *DSM-IV*, and various social skills that parents and caregivers can teach as part of a Treatment Plan for each disorder. The various disorders and charts are broken into two sections: The first section contains charts on disorders that the *DSM-IV* categorizes as Axis I disorders, while the second section presents charts on disorders that are categorized as Axis II disorders.

Examples of Treatment Plans for the youth described in the various settings – school, residential group home, and psychiatric facility – in the three examples at the beginning of the book are included in Chapter 5. These examples demonstrate how social skills can be integrated into a youth's overall Treatment Plan for particular *DSM-IV* diagnoses across different settings and levels of care.

5

Finally, the Appendix presents a brief description of the programs that make up Boys Town's Continuum of Care, along with Boys Town's philosophy of care, which is at the heart of each and every one of its programs.

Of course, only qualified professionals who have had the proper schooling, clinical training, and experience should use the *DSM-IV* to evaluate and diagnose youth who may have a mental health disorder. An accurate *DSM-IV* diagnosis of a troubled youth's disorder enables caregivers across the entire spectrum of treatment settings (e.g., schools, shelters, residential treatment programs, psychiatric treatment settings, and so on) to provide better, more therapeutic treatment.

We hope you find this book useful in your work with children and adolescents. All youth must learn social skills in order to find success in their lives; teaching these social skills as part of treatment for a mental health disorder truly can enhance a child's progress and help him or her to overcome problems.

Chapter 1

History of the DSM-IV

The initial impetus for developing a classification of mental health disorders was the collection of statistical information for the U.S. Census back in 1840. At that time, there was one crude category for such disorders – "idiocy/insanity." By the 1880 census, there were seven categories of mental illnesses. This gathering of statistical information on mental health disorders continued until 1952. That's when the first edition of the *Diagnostic and Statistical Manual: Mental Disorders* (or *DSM-I*) was published by the American Psychiatric Association. This manual contained a glossary of descriptions of the diagnostic categories and was the first official manual of mental health disorders designed for clinical use. Shortly thereafter, the *DSM-II*, which contained a new round of diagnostic revisions, was published. The *DSM-III* followed in 1980. It introduced a number of important methodological innovations and a descriptive approach that attempted to be neutral with respect to the theories of etiology. In 1987, the American Psychiatric Association published the *DSM-III-R*, which contained revisions and corrections for inconsistencies and instances where criteria were not entirely clear in the *DSM-III*.

The *DSM-IV* came about due to the substantial increase in research that was generated by the *DSM-III* and *DSM-III-R*.

By that time, most diagnoses had empirical literature or available data sets. So, according to the *DSM-IV*, its current content is based on "comprehensive and systematic reviews of published literature, reanalysis of already collected data sets, and extensive issue-focused field trials." The *DSM-IV* currently includes 340 mental health disorders, nearly 120 more than the *DSM-III-R*. Obviously, there are probably still more conditions out there, waiting to be discovered.

DSM-IV and Other Assessment Tools

According to the *Diagnostic and Statistical Manual of Mental Disorders (DSM-IV)*, "the utility and credibility of the *DSM-IV* require that it focus on its clinical, research, and educational purposes and be supported by an extensive empirical foundation." However, the most important function of the *DSM-IV* is to serve as a helpful guide for mental health professionals as they evaluate and diagnose patients with psychiatric disorders. The *DSM-IV* goes on to state: "The specific diagnostic criteria included in the *DSM-IV* are meant to serve as guidelines to be informed by clinical judgment and are not meant to be used in a cookbook fashion. For example, the exercise of clinical judgment may justify giving a certain diagnosis to an individual even though the clinical presentation falls just short of meeting the full criteria for the diagnosis." In other words, evaluating and diagnosing youth with mental health disorders is not an exact science, and the use of the *DSM-IV* does not guarantee a completely accurate diagnosis – it also requires the use of judgment, expertise, and experience. But, competently utilizing the *DSM-IV* during the evaluation process greatly enhances the chances of making an accurate diagnosis. This obviously can lead to better, more successful treatment.

Parents and caregivers spend a tremendous amount of time with youth in the various treatment environments. Thus, it also is important for them to become aware and knowledgeable of some of the more prevalent *DSM-IV* diagnoses for children and adolescents. Gaining an insight and understanding of these diagnoses can help parents and caregivers to communicate more effectively with a child's psychiatrist, psychologist, or therapist. As a result, all those involved in the youth's treatment (i.e., "treatment team") will have a much better opportunity to develop a successful Treatment Plan that incorporates appropriate social skills and treatment goals.

The *DSM-IV* is generally one of the first evaluation tools utilized by trained and knowledgeable mental health professionals to accurately diagnose mental health disorders. Other information can come from youth interviews, psychological testing, parent reports, school reports, cultural and ethnic factors, etc. The use of these methods allows mental health professionals to gather more detailed information about a youth's problem, thus helping to strengthen the accuracy of the evaluation and diagnostic process.

Another important evaluation tool widely used by mental health professionals – in concert with the *DSM-IV* – is the Diagnostic Interview Schedule for Children (DISC). This is a structured interview for children and adolescents that allows mental health professionals to obtain diagnostic criteria information for common psychiatric disorders. Friman (1997) says that DISC data "provides information on the kinds of psychological problems exhibited by youth" entering various treatment environments and that "the value of this information is most apparent in treatment planning."

A third assessment tool is the Child Behavior Checklist (CBCL). According to Achenbach (1991), "The CBCL is designed to record in a standardized format children's competencies and problems as reported by their parents or parent surrogates." It contains 118 questions for assessing behavioral/emotional problems that are of concern to parents and mental health professionals. Achenbach (1991) states that, "The value of this assessment tool lies in the understanding that parents (and parent surrogates) are typically among the most important sources of data about children's competencies and problems. They are usually the most knowledgeable about their child's behavior across time and situations. Furthermore, parental involvement is required in the evaluation of most children, and parents' views of their children's behavior are often crucial in determining what will be done about behavior" (i.e., Treatment Plan development).

The CBCL also is one of the most commonly used tools in evaluating and measuring the effectiveness of a child's treatment. This can be done by administering the test before the child enters a program and when he or she leaves the program. If the child's overall score on the CBCL is lower when he or she leaves than it was when he or she arrived, it is an excellent indicator that the child's behavioral/emotional problems have diminished and that treatment was effective. (See Chapter 3, "Social Skills and *DSM-IV* Mental Health Disorders" for more on this issue.)

Using evaluation tools like the DISC and CBCL can contribute to more accurate diagnoses of *DSM-IV* disorders and enables the treatment team to begin developing therapeutic, effective Treatment Plans for youth.

The Use of Multiaxial Assessment

In order to arrive at an accurate *DSM-IV* diagnosis, and ultimately provide successful treatment, an effective evaluation process is necessary. One widely recognized procedure for evaluating an individual with a mental health disorder is the multiaxial assessment system detailed in the *DSM-IV*. In this process, mental health professionals obtain comprehensive information about different domains in a person's life, then examine this information during the evaluation process to help them achieve the most precise *DSM-IV* disorder diagnosis possible.

The *DSM-IV* multiaxial assessment system includes:

Axis I   Clinical Disorders
Other Conditions That May Be a Focus of Clinical Attention

Axis II   Personality Disorders
Mental Retardation

Axis III   General Medical Conditions

Axis IV   Psychosocial and Environmental Problems

Axis V   Global Assessment of Functioning

Simply put, Axis I and Axis II are two separate classifications that contain all the various mental health disorders in the *DSM-IV*. The disorders grouped and reported as Axis I are classified by the *DSM-IV* as "Clinical Disorders" or "Other Conditions That May Be a Focus of Clinical Attention," while the disorders grouped and reported as Axis II are classified by the *DSM-IV* as "Personality Disorders" or "Mental Retardation."

The focus of Axis III is reporting any current general medical conditions that might be relevant to the understanding or management of an individual's mental health disorder. An example of this, according to the *DSM-IV*, would be when "hypothyroidism is a direct cause of depressive symptoms." The *DSM-IV* says that "Axis IV is for reporting psychosocial and environmental problems that may affect diagnosis, treatment, and prognosis" of a *DSM-IV* disorder (e.g., divorce, death of a family member, job loss, being a crime victim, and so on).

Finally, Axis V summarizes a mental health professional's judgment of an individual's overall level of functioning on the Global Assessment of Functioning (GAF) scale. The GAF scale can be used at admission, at various times during treatment, and at discharge. The use of this scale can be extremely beneficial in treatment planning and in measuring the success of treatment over time.

According to the *DSM-IV*, "a multiaxial system provides a convenient format for organizing and communicating clinical information, for capturing the complexity of clinical situations, and for describing the heterogeneity of individuals presenting with the same diagnosis. In addition, the multiaxial system promotes the application of the biopsychosocial approach model in clinical, educational, and research settings." It is a comprehensive and systematic evaluation system that allows a mental health professional to take into account all aspects of a person's life that might be contributing to the problem instead of focusing on a single presenting problem. In the end, this extensive evaluation process greatly enhances a mental health professional's diagnostic capabilities.

Summary

The *DSM-IV* has evolved from a mere collection of statistical information for the U.S. Census in 1840 to being the world's standard tool for evaluating and diagnosing mental health disorders in children, adolescents, and adults. Other assessment tools that have been developed to be used in conjunction with the *DSM-IV* include the DISC, the CBCL, and the multiaxial assessment system described in the *DSM-IV*. Besides providing mental health professionals with more comprehensive information during the evaluation process, these tools also help produce thorough evaluations that lead to more accurate diagnoses. This enables caregivers to create and develop therapeutic, successful Treatment Plans for youth requiring treatment.

Chapter 2

Culture and Ethnicity in Treating DSM-IV Disorders

One of the greatest improvements in the *DSM-IV* over the years has been the recognition of the important role a person's cultural and ethnic background plays in the accurate evaluation, diagnosis, and treatment of mental health disorders. Gaw (1994) states: "Cultural concepts, values, and beliefs shape the way mental symptoms are expressed and how individuals and their families respond to such distress. Cultural norms dictate when a cluster of symptoms and behaviors are labeled 'normal' or 'abnormal.' Clearly, effective mental health care cannot be divorced from the cultural context in which the formation and expression of psychic distress occur; the coping strategies of the patients and their families and communities; and the diagnostic and therapeutic activities of the 'healers.'"

The *DSM-IV* recognizes that professionals who are trained in evaluating and diagnosing children and adolescents for psychiatric disorders need to take into account cultural and ethnic factors. The *DSM-IV* says: "Diagnostic assessment can be especially challenging when a clinician from one ethnic or cultural group uses the *DSM-IV* Classification to evaluate an individual from a different ethnic or cultural group. A clinician who is unfamiliar with the nuances of an individual's cultural frame of reference may incorrectly judge as psychopathology these normal variations in behavior, belief, or experience that are particular to the individual's culture. For example, certain religious spiritual practices (e.g., hearing or seeing a deceased relative during bereavement) may be misdiagnosed as manifestations of a Psychotic Disorder." Therefore, "special efforts have been made in the preparation of *DSM-IV* to incorporate an awareness that the manual is used in culturally diverse populations in the United States and internationally."

Addressing Cultural Diversity

The *DSM-IV* addresses the issue of cultural diversity in three ways. First, there is a section in the text that discusses specific cultural issues or factors that should be considered when evaluating and diagnosing certain *DSM-IV* disorders. Second, an outline that can assist clinicians when they consider a person's cultural and ethnic background during the assessment period is included in the appendix. Finally, the appendix also contains a glossary of some of the more well-known and best-studied culture-bound syndromes that may be encountered when working with individuals from particular cultures.

As you can see, the *DSM-IV* places tremendous emphasis on the role culture plays in the evaluation of individuals for mental health disorders. Only in this way can professionals arrive at a responsible and accurate diagnosis of a person's problem. Once a diagnosis is made, it is equally important that cultural issues be part of treatment.

With social skill instruction as part of a Treatment Plan, cultural and ethnic factors will influence how and what social skills are selected, how these social skills are taught, and what skill components will be included. For example, many Native American cultures consider it a sign of disrespect for a child to make direct eye contact with an adult. But almost all the social skills taught in the Boys Town Teaching Model include the component, "Look at the person." Therefore, when teaching this specific behavior to Native American children, you may

14

need to modify or target it for extra teaching and shape it over a longer period of time. You also should teach discrimination skills to Native American children, helping them to understand that it is acceptable to look at their teacher at school or boss at work, but not appropriate to make eye contact with elders in their own culture.

According to Glomb (1996), teachers who work with culturally diverse youth should recognize and make accommodations in their social skill instruction and curricula in the classroom for these kinds of differences. Boys Town believes this same standard should exist in all the settings where troubled youth receive treatment. Further, Glomb developed a list of 23 questions that can serve as a "method of analyzing the cultural responsiveness" of social skills curricula. These questions can be an excellent resource and guide for caregivers in different treatment environments as they create social skill curricula that are effective and therapeutic for youth from all cultures.

Summary

In order to competently and successfully evaluate, diagnose, and treat children and adolescents from various cultures who have *DSM-IV* disorders, it is imperative for all caregivers – from the professionals who evaluate and diagnose the *DSM-IV* disorder to the staff members or parents who provide treatment to the youth – to take into account the youth's cultural and ethnic background. The *DSM-IV* goes to great lengths to provide mental health professionals with information and guidelines about cultural factors they can use during the evaluation process to help them achieve an accurate diagnosis. Once this diagnosis is made, it is up to the treatment team to create and adapt strategies to fit the needs of each and every youth. Only in this way can caregivers truly provide responsible, successful treatment.

Chapter 3

Social Skills and DSM-IV Mental Health Disorders

Boys Town believes that social skill instruction is an integral element in successfully treating youth with mental health and/or behavioral disorders. This belief is based on vast experience, successful treatment outcomes, and comprehensive research that shows that children and adolescents do get better when they learn prosocial skills.

This chapter will provide an overview of the Boys Town Teaching Model and its Social Skill Curriculum. In addition, there will be an examination of the effectiveness of social skill instruction as part of treatment for youth in various levels of care. We also will discuss how *DSM-IV* diagnoses can help determine which social skills to target for teaching and what goals to set for treatment.

Overview of the Boys Town Teaching Model

While the Boys Town Teaching Model has its basis in learning theory, it has not adopted a "mechanistic" view of how a child learns, as have other models that take this approach. In the Boys Town Model, the child is an active participant in the teaching and learning that occurs. The child isn't merely told how to behave; he or she learns positive behaviors and how to choose to use them in many different situations. This "empowerment," or self-help, approach combines the active participation of the child with the active teaching of the parent or caretaker. The strength of this approach is that it teaches children positive social skills and helps them build healthy relationships with others. Subsequently, the overall goal of the Boys Town Teaching Model is to teach a child how to learn self-help skills and build positive relationships, both of which result in intrinsic changes within the child.

By learning self-help skills, children can change the way they think, feel, and act. This is a learning process. Boys Town's teaching methods utilize behavioral principles, while allowing children to integrate their thoughts and feelings into this learning process. And unlike many other learning theory models, Boys Town uses external reinforcement, where appropriate, to promote and maintain skill-learning and relationship development. This enables children to change intrinsically. Inadequate thought patterns change, negative feelings diminish, and inappropriate behaviors are replaced by positive behaviors, which benefits the youth and others. (For a more detailed description of the Boys Town Teaching Model, see *Issues in Quality Child Care*, published by the Boys Town Press.)

Why Kids Misbehave

Youth require intervention and treatment for many reasons. According to the Boys Town philosophy, one of the most influential factors in the development of behavioral and mental health problems is that youth have not yet learned the social skills needed to overcome the problems in their lives. In most cases, when troubled youth require treatment, the environments they come from have significantly contributed to and fostered the formation of problem behaviors and mental health difficulties. However, these learned inappropriate behaviors and skills serve a purpose; they enable the youth to get what he or she needs and wants. Over time, these same behaviors and skills become reinforced and strengthened, and eventually spill over to other environments (e.g., school, sports teams, jobs, relationships with peers and adults, and so on). In these new settings, youth try to use the same negative behaviors that were successful for them in the past; when they don't work, kids flounder, not knowing what it takes to be successful. So, in order for youth to succeed in previous and new environments, situations, and relationships, they must learn new prosocial skills that will help them get their needs met in ways that are more socially acceptable.

Social Skill Teaching

Boys Town's social skill instruction approach to treatment focuses on teaching the essential life skills young people need in order to make the successful transition into young adulthood (Peter, 1986). Social, academic, and vocational skills, as well as spiritual values, are taught in a "family-style" treatment setting through proactively teaching at neutral times, reinforcing positive behavior as it occurs, practicing and rehearsing, correcting inappropriate behavior in a positive style, and helping youth learn to use alternative appropriate behaviors when they face crisis situations.

According to Combs and Slaby (1977), a social skill can be defined as "the ability to interact with others in a given social context in specific ways that are socially acceptable or valued and, at the same time, personally beneficial, mutually beneficial, or beneficial primarily to others." Thus, social skills are sets of behaviors that do not remain constant, but vary with the social context and particular situational demands. These skills not only produce positive consequences for the individual, but also are socially acceptable and responsive to others.

Boys Town's Social Skill Curriculum contains 182 skills that address a wide variety of youth issues at all levels, from minor school- or home-related problems to more serious problems like aggression, delinquency, depression, and suicide. This Social Skill Curriculum provides youth with positive alternatives to many of the maladaptive and self-defeating behavior patterns that entangle them.

With social skill instruction, youth learn skills that are determined to be the most functional for them and produce the best long-term results. This means that

19

every youth requires individual treatment. Some youngsters will initially need to learn the most basic skills (e.g., Following Instructions, Accepting Consequences, Accepting "No" Answers, etc.) in order to lay a foundation for more complex skills (e.g., Expressing Feelings Appropriately, Resisting Peer Pressure, Spontaneous Problem-Solving, etc.). Many times, parents and caregivers will need to gradually shape a youth's behavior by patiently teaching basic social skills so that the youth can learn the final desired behavior. This can be a slow, arduous process for caregivers and youth, but it is necessary if the youth is to overcome his or her problems.

The use of appropriate social skills involves an immensely complex chain of rapidly occurring interpersonal events. For youth, especially those suffering from mental health disorders that dramatically limit their emotional and cognitive functioning, correctly performing these skills at the right time can be an overwhelming task. They have considerable difficulty organizing and blending their behaviors into smooth-flowing interactions with others, particularly under stressful conditions. So, parents and caregivers must be able and willing to adjust their teaching techniques, vocabulary, and interpersonal behaviors to best meet the learning style of each youth in their care.

When choosing social skills for treatment, it is important for parents and caregivers to take into account individual factors like the age and developmental level of the youth, severity of the youth's behaviors, the length of time a youth has been exposed to social skill instruction, and so on. These factors play a pivotal role in the success or failure of each youth's Treatment Plan. Once the most appropriate skills have been identified and prioritized, parents and caregivers can utilize the various Teaching Interactions (e.g., Proactive Teaching, Effective Praise, Corrective Teaching, and Crisis Teaching) developed at Boys Town to reinforce and teach youth new prosocial ways of getting their needs met.

All 182 curriculum skills, the steps to each skill, and the Teaching Interactions that form the cornerstone of treatment planning and active intervention at Boys Town are presented in Boys Town's manual,

Teaching Social Skills to Youth, A Curriculum for Child-Care Providers. The Social Skill Curriculum and teaching techniques described in that book can be easily integrated into a variety of settings (e.g., natural home environment, emergency shelter care program, group home residential program, psychiatric treatment program, and others).

An Effective Treatment Strategy

Over the years, Boys Town has shown through research that one valuable and effective treatment strategy for children and adolescents with mental health disorders involves teaching them appropriate social skills. Dowd and Tierney (1992) state; "The philosophy within the Boys Town program regarding social skill instruction is that problem behaviors demonstrated by a youth are viewed as deficits in the youth's repertoire of these skills and that active, direct teaching is a key to remediation and growth. Positive, prosocial behaviors can be modeled, taught, and rewarded, and, therefore, become viable alternatives for the youth when he or she is confronted with situations that previously resulted in getting into trouble."

How do we know that social skill instruction – one of the hallmarks of the Boys Town Teaching Model – is a therapeutic, effective treatment strategy?

One way to answer this question is to compare the total scores obtained from the Child Behavior Checklist (CBCL) for youth when they enter a program to their scores when they leave. As mentioned earlier, this is an excellent and widely used measure of whether youth behavior/emotional problems get better or worse over the course of treatment. The chart on page 22 (Thompson & Teare, 1998) shows this data across five programs on the Boys Town Continuum of Care, which will be discussed in the Appendix. (The CBCL data was acquired from records of all the youth served in these five programs during 1996.) In all five Boys Town programs, the total CBCL scores dropped dramatically from admission to departure, indicating that youth behavior/emotional problems decreased and got better.

Is Care Effective?
CBCL Chart Across Programs at Admission & Departure (1996)

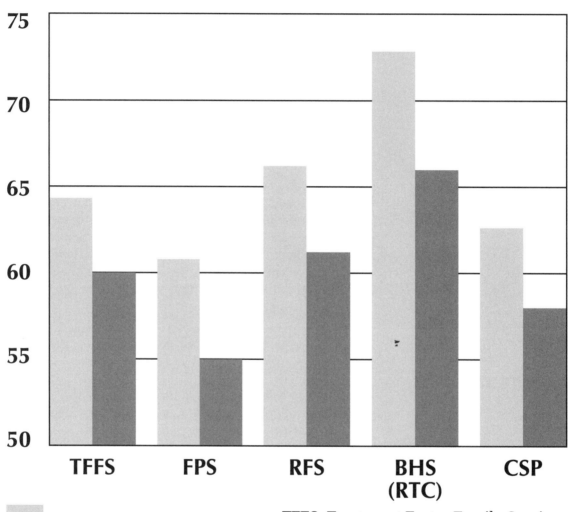

Total Score at Admission

Total Score at Departure

TFFS: Treatment Foster Family Services
FPS: Family Preservation Services
RFS: Residential Family Services
BHS: (RTC) Behaviorial Health Services
    (Residential Treatment Center)
CSP: Common Sense Parenting®

• A T-score is a standardized score where "normal" is considered at a score of 60 or below.
• Borderline clinical range: 60-63
• Clinical range: 64+

Another way to address this question is to look at what kind of environment youth go to once they leave a program. Data on page 24 (Thompson & Teare, 1998) shows that an overwhelming percentage of youth served in the four Boys Town programs that were measured move to a less-restrictive setting on the continuum once they finish treatment. (This data was obtained from records on all the youth served in the four programs during 1996.) This also is a very strong indicator that youth are getting better during treatment and that their behavior/emotional problems are diminishing.

Such data strongly suggests that kids are getting better when they receive treatment in the various Boys Town programs, all of which incorporate social skill instruction as one of the primary treatment strategies. We believe this verifies that social skill instruction is a proven, effective, and therapeutic treatment option.

Just as other strategies (psychotropic medication; individual or group therapy with a psychologist, counselor, therapist, or social worker) are prescribed as part of a youth's Treatment Plan, so too are the specific social skills that youth need to learn.

Boys Town has developed a series of reference charts that list possible skills that can be taught for certain *DSM-IV* disorders prevalent during childhood and adolescence. (These charts will be introduced and explained in the next chapter.) The skills are chosen on the basis of the behaviors that make up the skill and how they match up with the symptoms and behaviors of each disorder. In other words, they best address the symptomology and provide alternative behaviors to replace the negative behaviors that manifest the disorders.

Summary

The core of the Boys Town Teaching Model involves building relationships and teaching social skills. The Model incorporates a social skill instruction approach – teaching youth positive alternative skills to replace negative behaviors – while also recognizing the importance and need for other types of treatment strategies, like medications and therapy, as important ingredients to an overall Treatment Plan. Equally

Is Care Effective?
Percentage of Youth in Out-of-Home Placements Discharged to a Less-Restrictive Setting (1996)

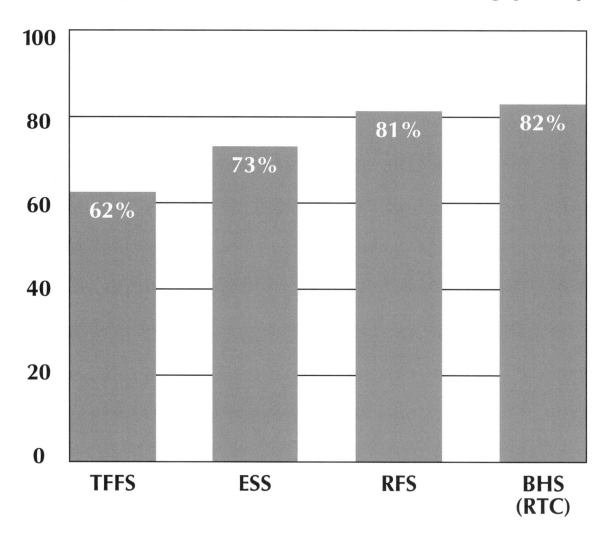

TFFS: Treatment Foster Family Services
ESS: Emergency Shelter Services
RFS: Residential Family Services
BHS: (RTC) Behaviorial Health Services
   (Residential Treatment Center)

important to successful treatment planning are prescribing and assigning suitable social skills for targeted teaching by parents and caregivers. Boys Town's extensive research has shown that social skill instruction, in a wide variety of treatment settings, is a valuable and effective treatment option for helping troubled youth overcome their problems.

Chapter 4

Axis I and Axis II DSM-IV Disorders and Social Skills Charts

As mentioned earlier, all the mental health disorders contained in the *DSM-IV* are grouped into one of two categories: Axis I disorders and Axis II disorders. Axis I disorders are those reported by the *DSM-IV* as "Clinical Disorders" and "Other Conditions That May Be a Focus of Clinical Attention." The disorders listed as Axis II disorders are those reported by the *DSM-IV* as "Personality Disorders" and "Mental Retardation."

This chapter is divided into two sections. The first section contains a series of 35 charts on Axis I *DSM-IV* disorders, while the second section contains eight charts on Axis II *DSM-IV* disorders. The various disorders listed in each section are those that are commonly diagnosed for children and adolescents, and the names of the disorders are as they appear in the *DSM-IV*. The disorders for these charts were chosen by a panel of youth-care experts at Boys Town; the charts do not include every *DSM-IV* disorder.

The first column of the chart, labeled "Diagnostic Criteria," lists specific criteria (as they appear in the *DSM-IV*) that a trained mental health professional would use when evaluating a youth for a specific mental health disorder. A diagnosis would be based in part on whether a youth meets the listed evaluation criteria. Keep in mind that in order to formulate a specific diagnosis, and subsequently, a successful Treatment Plan, mental health professionals will invariably require considerable additional information from other sources. Interviews with the youth, psychological tests, parent reports, school reports, cultural and ethnic factors, and other sources all play an important role during an evaluation.

The second column of the chart – "Possible Skills" – presents social skills that parents and other caregivers could select and target for teaching for a particular disorder. It is important to remember that treatment planning – including determining which of the social skills to teach – should be individualized to meet the needs of each child. Even when youth are diagnosed with the same disorder, the specific social skills they should learn might be different. Usually, the treatment team will choose skills that address a child's greatest skill-deficit areas and provide the most therapeutic value to the overall treatment goals. For example, two youth may be diagnosed with Posttraumatic Stress Disorder. But after a thorough evaluation, the treatment team might recommend teaching the social skill of "Expressing Optimism" to one youth, and teaching the skill of "Resisting Peer Pressure" to the other youth.

These charts are presented as a guide for mental health professionals who develop Treatment Plans that include social skill instruction as a strategy for treating youth with a mental health disorder. By using these charts, treatment teams can more easily and efficiently develop and prescribe social skills that are appropriate for a specific diagnosis and individually suited to meet each child's treatment goals.

Axis I Disorders

Clinical Disorders
and
*Other Disorders That May Be
a Focus of Clinical Attention*

ADJUSTMENT DISORDERS

Diagnostic Criteria

A) Emotional or behavioral symptoms in response to an identifiable stressor occurring within three months of the onset of the stressor

B) Symptoms or behaviors are clinically significant as evidenced by either of the following:

  (1) marked distress that is in excess of what would be expected from exposure to the stressor

  (2) significant impairment in social or occupational (academic) functioning

C) Does not meet the criteria for another disorder and is not merely an exacerbation of a pre-existing disorder

D) Symptoms do not represent bereavement

E) Once the stressor (or its consequences) has terminated, the symptoms do not persist more than an additional six months

Possible Skills

Asking for Help

Assertiveness

Conversation Skills

Expressing Emotions

Expressing Opinions

Greeting/Departure Skills

Participating in Activities

Goal-Setting

Positive Statements

Relaxation

Structured Problem-Solving

AGORAPHOBIA

Diagnostic Criteria

A) Anxiety about being in places or situations from which escape might be difficult (or embarrassing) or in which help may not be available in the event of having an unexpected or situationally predisposed panic attack or panic-like symptoms. Agoraphobic fears typically involve characteristic clusters of situations that include being outside the home alone; being in a crowd or standing in a line; being on a bridge; and traveling in a bus, train, or automobile

B) The situations are avoided (e.g., travel is restricted) or else are endured with marked distress or with anxiety about having a panic attack or panic-like symptoms, or require the presence of a companion

C) The anxiety or phobic avoidance is not better accounted for by another mental disorder, such as social phobia, specific phobia, obsessive-compulsive disorder, posttraumatic stress disorder, or separation anxiety disorder

Possible Skills

Interacting with Others
Asking for Help
Relaxation Techniques
Identifying Emotions
Expressing Emotions
Participating in Activities
Time Management
Structured Problem-Solving
Self-Talk or Instruction
Monitoring Self
Seeking Professional Assistance
Dealing with Fear
Conversation Skills
Greeting and Departure Skills
Assertiveness
Goal-Setting
Positive Statements
Controlling Emotions
Preparing for Stressful Events

ATTENTION-DEFICIT/HYPERACTIVITY DISORDER

Diagnostic Criteria

A) Either (1) or (2):

(1) six (or more) of the following symptoms of inattention have persisted for at least six months to a degree that is maladaptive and inconsistent with developmental level:

Inattention

    (a) often fails to give close attention to details or makes careless mistakes in schoolwork, work, or other activities

    (b) often has difficulty sustaining attention in tasks or play activities

    (c) often does not seem to listen when spoken to directly

    (d) often does not follow through on instructions and fails to finish schoolwork, chores, or duties in the workplace (not due to oppositional behavior or failure to understand instructions)

    (e) often has difficulties organizing tasks or activities

    (f) often avoids, dislikes, or is reluctant to engage in tasks that require sustained mental effort (such as schoolwork or homework)

    (g) often loses things necessary for tasks or activities (e.g., toys, school assignments, pencils, books, or tools)

    (h) is often easily distracted by extraneous stimuli

    (i) is often forgetful in daily activities

(2) six (or more) of the following symptoms of hyperactivity-impulsivity have persisted for at least six months to a

(Continued on next page)

Possible Skills

Following Instructions
Accepting "No" Answers
Accepting Criticism
Accepting Consequences
Completing Homework
Appropriate Voice Tone
Completing Tasks
Contributing to Discussions
Getting Other Person's Attention
Getting the Teacher's Attention
Good Quality of Work
Ignoring Distractions by Others
Listening to Others
Making a Request
Resisting Peer Pressure
Seeking Positive Attention
Staying on Task
Waiting Your Turn
Accepting Help or Assistance
Concentrating on Subject or Task
Dealing with Boredom
Dealing with Frustration
Delaying Gratification
Organizing Tasks and Activities
Persevering on Tasks and Projects
Responding to Teasing
Sharing Attention with Others
Study Skills
Time Management
Use of Appropriate Humor
Use of Appropriate Language
Goal-Setting
Patience
Planning Ahead
Stress Management

ATTENTION-DEFICIT/HYPERACTIVITY DISORDER (CONT.)

Diagnostic Criteria

(Continued from previous page)
degree that is maladaptive and inconsistent with developmental level:

Hyperactivity

(a) often fidgets with hands or feet or squirms in seat

(b) often leaves seat in classroom or in other situations in which remaining seated is expected

(c) often runs about or climbs excessively in situations in which it is inappropriate (in adolescents or adults, may be limited to subjective feelings of restlessness)

(d) often has difficulty playing or engaging in leisure activities quietly

(e) is often "on the go" or often acts as if "driven by a motor"

(f) often talks excessively

Impulsivity

(g) often blurts out answers before questions have been completed

(h) often has difficulty awaiting turn

(i) often interrupts or intrudes on others (e.g., butts into conversations or games)

B) Some hyperactivity-impulsivity or inattentive symptoms that caused impairment were present before age seven years

C) Some impairment from the symptoms is present in two or more settings (e.g., at school or work, and at home)

D) There must be clear evidence of clinically significant impairment in school, academic, or occupational functioning

E) The symptoms do not occur excessively during the course of a pervasive developmental disorder, schizophrenia, or other psychotic disorder, and are not better accounted for by other mental disorders (e.g., mood disorder, anxiety disorder, dissociative disorder, or a personality disorder)

BIPOLAR I DISORDER

Diagnostic Criteria

A) Presence of only one manic episode and no past major depressive episodes

B) The manic episode is not better accounted for by schizoaffective disorder and is not superimposed on schizophrenia, schizo-phreniform disorder, delusional disorder, or psychotic disorder not otherwise specified

Specify if:

Mixed: if symptoms meet criteria for a mixed episode

Specify (for current or most recent episode):

Severity/Psychotic/Remission specifiers

With catatonic features

With postpartum onset

Possible Skills

Interacting with Others

Accepting Compliments

Accepting Self

Assertiveness

Coping with Change

Expressing Feelings

Optimism

Goal-Setting

Identifying Feelings

Managing Stress

Positive Self-Statements

Participating in Activities

Structured Problem-Solving

Requesting Help

Self-Monitoring and Reflection

Use of Leisure Time

Relaxation Strategies

Time Management

BIPOLAR II DISORDER

Diagnostic Criteria

A) Presence (or history) of one or more major depressive episodes

B) Presence (or history) of at least one hypomanic episode

C) There has never been a manic episode

D) The mood symptoms in Criteria A and B are not better accounted for by schizoaffective disorder and are not superimposed on schizophrenia, schizophreniform disorder, delusional disorder, or psychotic disorder not otherwise specified

E) The symptoms cause clinically significant distress or impairment in important areas of functioning specificity (current or most recent episode):

Hypomanic: if currently (or most recently) in a Hypomanic episode

Depressed: if currently (or most recently) in a major depressive episode

Specify for current or most recent major depressive episode only if it is the most recent type of mood episode:

Severity/Psychotic/Remission specifiers

Chronic

With catatonic features

With melancholic features

With atypical features

With postpartum onset

Specify:

Longitudinal course specifiers

With seasonal pattern

With rapid cycling

Possible Skills

Interacting with Others
Accepting Compliments
Accepting Self
Assertiveness
Coping with Change
Expressing Feelings
Optimism
Goal-Setting
Identifying Feelings
Managing Stress
Positive Self-Statements
Participating in Activities
Structured Problem-Solving
Requesting Help
Self-Monitoring and Reflection
Use of Leisure Time
Relaxation Strategies
Time Management

BODY DYSMORPHIC DISORDER

Diagnostic Criteria

A) Preoccupation with an imagined defect in appearance

B) Preoccupation causes clinically significant distress or impairment in important areas of functioning

C) Not better accounted for by another mental disorder

Possible Skills

Accepting Compliments
Positive Self-Statements
Appropriate Clothing
Participating in Activities
Making Friends
Expressing Feelings Appropriately
Self-Advocacy
Self-Talk or Instruction
Accepting Self
Assertiveness
Laughing at Oneself
Seeking Professional Assistance
Dealing with Embarrassment

BRIEF PSYCHOTIC DISORDER

Diagnostic Criteria

A) Presence of one (or more) number of the following symptoms:
- (1) delusions
- (2) hallucinations
- (3) disorganized speech
- (4) grossly disorganized or catatonic behavior

B) Duration of an episode of the disturbance is at least one day but less than one month, with eventual full return to premorbid level of functioning

C) Disturbance is not better accounted for by a mood disorder with psychotic features, schizoaffective disorder, or schizophrenia and is not due to the direct physiological effects of a substance or a general medical condition

Specify if:

With marked stressor(s): (brief reactive psychosis) if symptoms occur shortly after and apparently in response to events that, singly or together, would be markedly stressful to almost anyone in similar circumstances in the person's culture

Without marked stressor(s): if psychotic symptoms do *not* occur shortly after, or are not apparently in response to events that, singly or together, would be markedly stressful to almost anyone in similar circumstances in the person's culture

Possible Skills

Accepting Compliments
Asking for Help
Asking Questions
Contributing to Discussions
Participating in Activities
Positive Self-Statements
Willingness to Try New Tasks

CONDUCT DISORDER

Diagnostic Criteria

A) A repetitive and persistent pattern of behavior in which the basic rights of others or major age-appropriate societal norms or rules are violated, as manifested by the presence of three (or more) of the following criteria in the past 12 months, with at least one criterion present in the past six months:

Aggression toward people and animals

(1) often bullies, threatens, or intimidates others

(2) often initiates physical fights

(3) has used a weapon that can cause serious physical harm to others (e.g., a bat, brick, broken bottle, knife, gun)

(4) has been physically cruel to people

(5) has been physically cruel to animals

(6) has stolen while confronting a victim (e.g., mugging, purse-snatching, extortion, armed robbery)

(7) has forced someone into sexual activity

Destruction of property

(8) has deliberately engaged in fire-setting with the intention of causing serious damage

(9) has deliberately destroyed others' property (other than by fire-setting)

Deceitfulness or theft

(10) has broken into someone else's house, building, or car

(11) often lies to obtain goods or favors or to avoid obligations (i.e., "cons" others)

(Continued on next page)

Possible Skills

Following Instructions

Accepting Consequences

Accepting "No" Answers

Accepting Criticism

Anger Control Strategies

Listening to Others

Positive Self-Statements about Others

Compromising with Others

Controlling Emotions

Coping with Anger and Aggression from Others

Self-Monitoring and Reflection

Expressing Concern and Understanding for Others

Relaxation Strategies

Making Restitution

Seeking Positive Attention

Disagreeing Appropriately

Showing Sensitivity to Others

Asking for Help

Following Rules

Interrupting Appropriately

Making an Apology

Structured Problem-Solving

Dealing with Accusations

Dealing with Frustrations

Expressing Feeling Appropriately

Negotiating with Others

Problem-Solving a Disagreement

Assertiveness

Conflict Resolution

Accepting Decisions of Authority

Communicating Honestly

Keeping Property in Its Place

(Continued on next page)

CONDUCT DISORDER (CONT.)

Diagnostic Criteria

(Continued from previous page)

(12) has stolen items of nontrivial value without confronting a victim (e.g., shoplifting, but without breaking and entering; forgery)

Serious violations of rules

(13) often stays out at night despite parental prohibitions, beginning before age 13

(14) has run away from home overnight at least twice while living in parental or parental surrogate home (or once without returning for a lengthy period)

(15) is often truant from school, beginning before age 13 years

B) The disturbance in behavior causes clinically significant impairment in social, academic, or occupational functioning.

C) If the individual is age 18 years or older, criteria are not met for antisocial personality disorder

Possible Skills

(Continued from previous page)

Interacting Appropriately with the Opposite Sex

Waiting Your Turn

Showing Respect

Getting Teacher's Attention

Care for Others' Property

Controlling Impulse to Steal

Use of Appropriate Language

Making New Friends

CONVERSION DISORDER

Diagnostic Criteria

A) One or more symptoms or deficits affecting voluntary motor or sensory function that suggest a neurological or other general medical condition

B) Psychological facts are judged to be associated with the symptom or deficit because the initiation or exacerbation of the symptoms or deficit is preceded by conflicts or other stressors

C) The symptom or other deficit is not intentionally produced or feigned

D) The symptom or deficit cannot, after appropriate investigation, be fully explained by a general medical condition, or by the direct effects of a substance, or as a culturally sanctioned behavior or experience

E) The symptom or deficit causes clinically significant distress or impairment in social, occupational, or other important areas of functioning or warrants medical evaluation

F) The symptom or deficit is not limited to pain or sexual dysfunction, does not occur exclusively during the course of somatization disorder, and is not better accounted for by another mental disorder

Possible Skills

Relaxation Techniques

Participating in Activities

Engaging in Conversation

Appropriate Appearance

Asking for Help

Positive Self-Statements

Seeking Positive Attention

Laughing at Oneself

Self-Monitoring and Reflection

Self-Talk or Instruction

CYCLOTHYMIC DISORDER

Diagnostic Criteria

A) For at least two years, the presence of numerous periods with hypomanic symptoms and numerous periods with depressive symptoms that do not meet criteria for a major depressive episode (for children and adolescents the duration must be at least one year)

B) During the above period the person has not been without the symptoms in Criterion A for more than two months at a time

C) No major depressive episode, manic episode, or mixed episode has been present during the first two years of the disturbance

D) The symptoms of Criterion A are not better accounted for by schizoaffective disorder and are not superimposed on schizophrenia, schizophreniform disorder, delusional disorder, or a psychotic disorder not otherwise specified

E) The symptoms are not due to the direct physiological effects of a substance or a general medical condition

F) The symptoms cause clinically significant distress or impairment in important areas of functioning

Possible Skills

Interacting with Others
Accepting Compliments
Accepting Self
Assertiveness
Coping with Change
Expressing Feelings
Optimism
Goal-Setting
Identifying Feelings
Managing Stress
Positive Self-Statements
Participating in Activities
Structured Problem-Solving
Requesting Help
Self-Monitoring and Reflection
Use of Leisure Time
Relaxation Strategies
Time Management

DELUSIONAL DISORDER

Diagnostic Criteria

A) Nonbizarre delusions of at least one month's duration

B) Criterion A for schizophrenia has never been met

C) Apart from the impact of the delusion(s) or its ramifications, functioning is not markedly impaired and behavior is not obviously odd or bizarre

D) If mood episodes have occurred concurrently with delusions, their total duration has been brief relative to the duration of the delusional periods

E) Not due to the direct physiological effects of a substance or a general medical condition

TYPES:

Erotomanic type: delusions that another person, usually of higher status, is in love with the individual

Grandiose type: delusions of inflated worth, power, knowledge, identity, or special relationship to a deity or famous person

Jealous type: delusions that the individual's sexual partner is unfaithful

Persecutory type: delusions that the person is being malevolently treated in some way

Somatic type: delusions that the person has some physical defect or general medical condition

Mixed type: delusions characteristic of more than one of the above types but no one theme predominates

Unspecified type

Possible Skills

Interacting with Others
Expressing Feelings
Identifying Feelings
Participating in Activities
Self-Monitoring and Reflection
Relaxation
Managing Stress

DEPERSONALIZATION DISORDER

Diagnostic Criteria

A) Persistent or recurrent experiences of feeling detached from, and as if one is an outside observer of, one's mental processes or body (e.g., feeling like one is in a dream)

B) During the depersonalization experience, reality testing remains intact

C) The depersonalization causes clinically significant distress or impairment in important areas of functioning

D) The depersonalization experience does not occur exclusively during the course of another mental disorder, such as schizophrenia, panic disorder, acute stress disorder, or another dissociative disorder, and is not due to the direct physiological effects of a substance, or a general medical condition

Possible Skills

Relaxation Techniques
Self-Monitoring and Reflection
Spontaneous Problem-Solving
Stress Management
Self-Reporting Own Behavior
Expressing Optimism

DISSOCIATIVE AMNESIA

Diagnostic Criteria

A) The predominant disturbance is one or more episodes of inability to recall important personal information, usually of a traumatic or stressful nature, that is too extensive to be explained by ordinary forgetfulness

B) The disturbance does not occur exclusively during the course of dissociative identity disorder, dissociative fugue, posttraumatic stress disorder, acute stress disorder, or somatization disorder, and is not due to the direct physiological effects of a substance or a neurological or other general medical condition

C) The symptoms cause clinically significant distress or impairment in important areas of functioning

Possible Skills

Asking for Help

Seeking Professional Assistance

Conversation Skills

Greeting and Departure Skills

Assertiveness

Stress Management

Relaxation Techniques

DISSOCIATIVE FUGUE

Diagnostic Criteria

A) The predominant disturbance is sudden, unexpected travel away from home or one's customary place of work, with inability to recall one's past

B) Confusion about personal identity or assumption of a new identity (partial or complete)

C) The disturbance does not occur exclusively during the course of dissociative identity disorder and is not due to the direct physiological effects of a substance or a general medical condition

D) The symptoms cause clinically significant distress or impairment in important areas of functioning

Possible Skills

Relaxation Techniques
Stress Management

DISSOCIATIVE IDENTITY DISORDER

Diagnostic Criteria

A) The presence of two or more distinct identities or personality states (each with its own relatively enduring pattern of perceiving, relating to, and thinking about the environment and self)

B) At least two of these identities or personality states recurrently take control of the person's behavior

C) Inability to recall important personal information that is too extensive to be explained by ordinary forgetfulness

D) The disturbance is not due to the direct physiological effects of a substance or a general medical condition (In children, the symptoms are not attributable to imaginary playmates or other fantasy play)

Possible Skills

Asking for Help

Conversation Skills

Relaxation Techniques

Appropriate Appearance

Assertiveness

Self-Monitoring and Reflection

Asking for Help or Assistance

Analyzing Skills Needed
    for Different Situations

Self-Reporting Own Behavior

Spontaneous Problem-Solving

DYSTHYMIC DISORDER

Diagnostic Criteria

A) Depressed mood for most of the day, for more days than not, as indicated either by subjective account or observation by others, for at least two years (in children and adolescents, mood can be irritable and duration must be at least one year)

B) Presence, while depressed, of two (or more) of the following:

(1) poor appetite or overeating

(2) insomnia or hypersomnia

(3) low energy or fatigue

(4) low self-esteem

(5) poor concentration or difficulty making decisions

(6) feelings of hopelessness

C) During the two-year period (one year for children and adolescents) of the disturbance, the person has never been without the symptoms in Criteria A and B for more than two months at a time

D) No major depressive episode has been present during the first two years of the disturbance (one year for children and adolescents); i.e., the disturbance is not better accounted for by chronic major depressive disorder, or major depressive disorder, in partial remission

E) There has never been a manic episode, a mixed episode, or a hypomanic episode, and criteria have never been met for cyclothymic disorder

F) The disturbance does not occur exclusively during the course of a chronic psychotic disorder, such as schizophrenia or delusional disorder

(Continued on next page)

Possible Skills

Interacting with Others
Accepting Compliments
Accepting Self
Assertiveness
Coping with Change
Expressing Feelings
Optimism
Goal-Setting
Identifying Feelings
Managing Stress
Positive Self-Statements
Participating in Activities
Structured Problem-Solving
Requesting Help
Self-Monitoring and Reflection
Relaxation
Use of Leisure Time
Dealing with Failure
Coping with Conflict
Accepting Defeat or Loss
Seeking Professional Assistance
Coping with Anger and Aggression
    from Others
Saying "No" Assertively
Self-Talk or Instruction

DYSTHYMIC DISORDER (CONT.)

Diagnostic Criteria

(Continued from previous page)

G) The symptoms are not due to the direct physiological effects of a substance or a general medical condition

H) The symptoms cause clinically significant distress or impairment in social, occupational, or other important areas of functioning

GENERALIZED ANXIETY DISORDER

Diagnostic Criteria

A) Excessive anxiety and worry occurring more days than not for a period of at least six months, about a number of events or activities

B) The individual finds it difficult to control the worry

C) Includes at least three additional symptoms from the following: restlessness, easily fatigued, difficulty concentrating or mind going blank, irritability, muscle tension, sleep disturbance

D) The focus of the anxiety and worry is not confined to feature of another Axis I disorder, and they do not occur exclusively during posttraumatic stress disorder

E) The individual reports subjective distress due to constant worry, difficulty controlling the worry, or experience-related impairment in other areas of function

F) The disturbance is not due to direct physiological effects or a substance or a general medical condition, and does not occur exclusively during a mood, psychotic, or pervasive developmental disorder

Possible Skills

Asking for Help
Stress Management
Interacting with Others
Participating in Activities
Patience
Expressing Emotions
Positive Statements
Identifying Feelings
Optimism
Goal-Setting
Self-Monitoring and Reflection
Use of Leisure Time

HYPOCONDRIASIS

Diagnostic Criteria

A) Preoccupation with fears of having or the idea that one has a serious disease, based on a misinterpretation of one or more bodily signs or symptoms

B) The belief is not of delusional intensity

C) The belief is also not restricted to a circumscribed concern about appearance, as seen in body dysmorphic disorder

D) The preoccupation with bodily symptoms causes clinically significant distress or impairment in important areas of functioning

E) The preoccupation lasts for at least six months

F) The preoccupation is not better accounted for by generalized anxiety disorder, obsessive-compulsive disorder, panic disorder, a major depressive episode, separation anxiety, or another somatoform disorder

Possible Skills

Greeting Others
Engaging in Conversation
Accepting Compliments
Appropriate Appearance
Positive Self-Statements
Expressing Feelings Appropriately
Coping with Change
Self-Advocacy
Self-Talk or Instruction
Accepting Self
Laughing at Oneself

INTERMITTENT EXPLOSIVE DISORDER

Diagnostic Criteria

A) Several discrete episodes of failure to resist aggressive impulses that result in serious assaultive acts or destruction of property

B) The degree of aggressiveness expressed during the episodes is grossly out of proportion to any precipitating psychosocial stressors

C) The aggressive episodes are not better accounted for by another mental disorder and are not due to the direct physiological effects of a substance or a general medical condition

Possible Skills

Anger Control
Accepting Criticism
Accepting "No" Answers
Appropriate Voice Tone
Dealing with Frustration
Delaying Gratification
Relaxation Strategies
Responding to Teasing
Self-Correcting Own Behaviors
Self-Talk or Instruction
Spontaneous Problem-Solving
Displaying Appropriate Control
Patience
Stress Management
Thought-Stopping

KLEPTOMANIA

Diagnostic Criteria

A) Recurrent failure to resist impulses to steal objects that are not needed for personal use or for their monetary value

B) Increasing sense of tension immediately before committing the theft

C) Pleasure, gratification, or relief at the time of committing the theft

D) The stealing is not committed to express anger or vengeance and is not in response to a delusion or a hallucination

E) The stealing is not better accounted for by conduct disorder, a manic episode, or antisocial personality disorder

Possible Skills

Reporting Whereabouts

Honesty

Delayed Gratification

Impulse Control

Making Restitution

Managing Stress

Moral Reasoning

Structured Problem-Solving

Respect for Property

Saying "No" Assertively

Self-Control

Self-Reporting

Thought-Stopping

Relaxation Strategies

Self-Correcting Own Behavior

Self-Talk or Instruction

MAJOR DEPRESSIVE DISORDER, RECURRENT

Diagnostic Criteria

A) Presence of two or more major depressive episodes

B) The major depressive episodes are not better accounted for by schizoaffective disorder, delusional disorder, or a psychotic disorder not otherwise specified

C) There has never been a manic episode, a mixed episode, or a hypomanic episode

Possible Skills

Interacting with Others
Accepting Compliments
Accepting Self
Assertiveness
Coping with Change
Expressing Feelings
Optimism
Goal-Setting
Grieving
Identifying Feelings
Managing Stress
Positive Self-Statements
Participating in Activities
Structured Problem-Solving
Requesting Help
Self-Monitoring and Reflection
Thought-Stopping
Use of Leisure Time
Self-Talk or Instruction
Coping with Change
Accepting Help or Assistance
Coping with Sad Feelings
Dealing with Fear
Expressing Pride in Accomplishments
Self-Advocacy
Self-Talk or Instruction
Appropriate Risk-Taking
Assessing Own Abilities
Identifying Own Feelings
Laughing at Oneself
Rewarding Yourself
Seeking Professional Assistance
Use of Leisure Time
Coping with Anger
Decision-Making

MAJOR DEPRESSIVE DISORDER, SINGLE EPISODE

Diagnostic Criteria

A) Presence of a single major depressive episode

B) The major depressive episode is not better accounted for by schizoaffective disorder and is not superimposed on schizophrenia, schizophreniform disorder, delusional disorder, or a psychotic disorder not otherwise specified

C) There has never been a manic episode, a mixed episode, or a hypomanic episode

Interacting with Others

Possible Skills

Accepting Compliments
Accepting Self
Assertiveness
Coping with Change
Expressing Feelings
Optimism
Goal-Setting
Grieving
Identifying Feelings
Managing Stress
Positive Self-Statements
Participating in Activities
Structured Problem-Solving
Requesting Help
Self-Monitoring and Reflection
Thought-Stopping
Use of Leisure Time
Self-Talk or Instruction
Coping with Change
Accepting Help or Assistance
Coping with Sad Feelings
Dealing with Fear
Expressing Pride in Accomplishments
Self-Advocacy
Self-Talk or Instruction
Appropriate Risk-Taking
Assessing Own Abilities
Identifying Own Feelings
Laughing at Oneself
Rewarding Yourself
Seeking Professional Assistance
Use of Leisure Time
Coping with Anger
Decision-Making

MAJOR DEPRESSIVE EPISODE

Diagnostic Criteria

A) Five (or more) of the following symptoms have been present during the same two-week period and represent a change from previous functioning; at least one of the symptoms is either (1) depressed mood or (2) loss of interest or pleasure

    (1) depressed mood most of the day, nearly every day, as indicated by either subjective report or observation made by others (in children and adolescents, can be irritable mood)

    (2) markedly diminished interest or pleasure in all, or almost all, activities most of the day, nearly every day (as indicated by either subjective account or observation made by others)

    (3) significant weight loss when not dieting or weight gain, or decrease or increase in appetite nearly every day (in children, consider failure to make expected weight gains)

    (4) insomnia or hypersomnia nearly every day

    (5) psychomotor agitation or retardation nearly every day (observable by others, not merely subjective feelings of restlessness or being slowed down)

    (6) fatigue or loss of energy nearly every day

    (7) feelings of worthlessness or excessive or inappropriate guilt (which may be delusional) nearly every day

    (8) diminished ability to think or concentrate, or indecisiveness, nearly every day, recurrent suicidal ideation without a specific plan, or a suicide attempt or a specific plan for committing suicide

(Continued on next page)

Possible Skills

Interacting with Others
Accepting Compliments
Accepting Self
Assertiveness
Coping with Change
Expressing Feelings
Optimism
Goal-Setting
Grieving
Identifying Feelings
Managing Stress
Positive Self-Statements
Participating in Activities
Structured Problem-Solving
Requesting Help
Self-Monitoring and Reflection
Thought-Stopping
Use of Leisure Time
Self-Talk or Instruction
Coping with Change
Accepting Help or Assistance
Coping with Sad Feelings
Dealing with Fear
Expressing Pride in Accomplishments
Self-Advocacy
Self-Talk or Instruction
Appropriate Risk-Taking
Assessing Own Abilities
Identifying Own Feelings
Laughing at Oneself
Rewarding Yourself
Seeking Professional Assistance
Use of Leisure Time
Coping with Anger
Decision-Making

MAJOR DEPRESSIVE EPISODE (CONT.)

Diagnostic Criteria

(Continued from previous page)

B) The symptoms do NOT meet criteria for a mixed episode

C) The symptoms cause clinically significant distress or impairment in social, occupational, or other important areas of functioning

D) The symptoms are NOT due to the direct physiological effects of a substance or a general medical condition

E) The symptoms are not better accounted for by bereavement (i.e., after the loss of a loved one), the symptoms persist for longer than two months or are characterized by marked functional impairment, morbid or preoccupation with worthlessness, suicidal ideation, psychotic symptoms, or psychomotor retardation

OBSESSIVE-COMPULSIVE DISORDER

Diagnostic Criteria

A) Recurrent obsessions or compulsions

B) The person has recognized they are excessive or unreasonable

C) Severe enough to be time-consuming or cause marked distress or significant impairment

D) If another disorder is present the obsessions/compulsions are not restricted to it

E) Not due to the direct physiological effects of a substance or general medical condition

Possible Skills

Dealing with Boredom

Dealing with Stress

Analyzing Tasks to Be Completed

Organizing Tasks and Activities

Self-Talk or Instruction

Spontaneous Problem-Solving

Self-Monitoring and Reflection

Displaying Appropriate Control

Stress Management

Thought-Stopping

Patience

Goal-Setting

Time Management

OPPOSITIONAL DEFIANT DISORDER

Diagnostic Criteria

A) A pattern of negativistic, hostile, and defiant behavior lasting at least six months, during which four (or more) of the following are present:

    (1) often loses temper

    (2) often argues with adults

    (3) often actively defies or refuses to comply with adults' requests or rules

    (4) often deliberately annoys people

    (5) often blames others for his or her mistakes or misbehavior

    (6) is often touchy or easily annoyed by others

    (7) is often angry and resentful

    (8) is often spiteful or vindictive

B) The disturbance in behavior causes clinically significant impairment in social, academic, or occupational functioning

C) The behaviors do not occur exclusively during the course of a psychotic or mood disorder

D) Criteria are not met for conduct disorder, and, if the individual is age 18 years or older, criteria are not met for antisocial personality disorder

Possible Skills

Following Instructions

Accepting Consequences

Accepting "No" Answers

Accepting Criticism

Anger Control Strategies

Listening to Others

Positive Self-Statements about Others

Compromising with Others

Controlling Emotions

Coping with Anger and Aggression from Others

Self-Monitoring and Reflection

Expressing Concern and Understanding for Others

Relaxation Strategies

Making Restitution

Seeking Positive Attention

Disagreeing Appropriately

Showing Sensitivity to Others

Asking for Help

Following Rules

Interrupting Appropriately

Making an Apology

Structured Problem-Solving

Dealing with Accusations

Dealing with Frustrations

Expressing Feeling Appropriately

Negotiating with Others

Problem-Solving a Disagreement

Assertiveness

Conflict Resolution

Accepting Decisions of Authority

Communicating Honestly

Keeping Property in Its Place

(Continued on next page)

OPPOSITIONAL DEFIANT DISORDER (CONT.)

Possible Skills

(Continued from previous page)

Interacting Appropriately with
   the Opposite Sex
Waiting Your Turn
Showing Respect
Getting Teacher's Attention
Care for Others' Property
Controlling Impulse to Steal
Use of Appropriate Language
Making New Friends

PAIN DISORDER

Diagnostic Criteria

A) Pain in one or more anatomical sites is the predominant focus of the clinical presentation and is of sufficient severity to warrant clinical attention

B) The pain causes clinically significant distress or impairment in important areas of functioning

C) Psychological factors are judged to have an important role in the onset, severity, exacerbation, or maintenance of the pain

D) The symptom or deficit is not intentionally produced or feigned

E) The pain is not better accounted for by a mood, anxiety, or psychotic disorder, and does not meet criteria for dyspareunia

Possible Skills

Anger Control Strategies

Asking for Help

Listening to Others

Controlling Emotions

Dealing with Frustration

Expressing Feelings Appropriately

Relaxation Strategies

Self-Correcting Own Behaviors

Conflict Resolution

Displaying Appropriate Control

Expressing Empathy and Understanding for Others

Self-Monitoring and Reflection

Laughing at Oneself

Stress Management

PANIC ATTACK

Diagnostic Criteria

A) A discrete period of intense fear or discomfort, in which four (or more) of the following symptoms developed abruptly and reached a peak within 10 minutes:

(1) palpitations, pounding heart, or accelerated heart rate
(2) sweating
(3) trembling or shaking
(4) sensations of shortness of breath or smothering
(5) feeling of choking
(6) chest pain or discomfort
(7) nausea or abdominal distress
(8) feeling dizzy, unsteady, lightheaded, or faint
(9) derealization (feelings of unreality) or depersonalization (being detached from oneself)
(10) fear of losing control or going crazy
(11) fear of dying
(12) parasthesias (numbness or tingling sensations)
(13) chills or hot flashes

Possible Skills

Interacting with Others
Asking for Help
Relaxation Techniques
Identifying Emotions
Expressing Emotions
Participating in Activities
Time Management
Structured Problem-Solving
Self-Talk or Instruction
Self-Monitoring and Reflection
Seeking Professional Assistance
Dealing with Fear
Preparing for a Stressful Event

POSTTRAUMATIC STRESS DISORDER

Diagnostic Criteria

A) The person has been exposed to a traumatic event in which both of the following were present:

(1) The person experienced, witnessed, or was confronted with an event or events that involved actual or threatened death or serious injury, or a threat to the physical integrity of self or others

(2) The person's response involved intense, fear, helplessness, or horror (Note: In children, this may be expressed instead by disorganized or agitated behavior)

B) The traumatic event is persistently re-experienced in one (or more) of the following ways:

(1) recurrent and intrusive distressing recollections of the event

(2) recurrent distressing dreams

(3) acting or feeling as if the traumatic event were recurring

(4) intense psychological distress at exposure to internal or external cues that symbolize or resemble an aspect of the traumatic event

(5) physiological reactivity on exposure to internal or external cues that symbolize or resemble an aspect of the traumatic event

C) Persistent avoidance of stimuli associated with the trauma and numbing of general responsiveness, as indicated by three (or more) of the following:

(1) efforts to avoid thoughts, feelings or conversations associated with the trauma

(Continued on next page)

Possible Skills

Relaxation
Asking for Help
Assertiveness
Expressing Emotions
Conversation Skills
Goal-Setting
Positive Statements
Structured Problem-Solving
Saying "No" Assertively
Resisting Peer Pressure
Seeking Positive Attention
Coping with Sad Feelings
Expressing Optimism
Expressing Pride in Accomplishments
Stress Management

POSTTRAUMATIC STRESS DISORDER (CONT.)

Diagnostic Criteria

(Continued from previous page)

(2) efforts to avoid activities, places, or people that arouse recollections of the trauma

(3) inability to recall an important aspect of the trauma

(4) markedly diminished interest or participation in significant activities

(5) feeling of detachment or estrangement from others

(6) restricted range of affect (e.g., unable to have loving feelings)

(7) sense of a foreshortened future

D) Persistent symptoms of increased arousal, as indicated by two (or more) of the following:

(1) difficulty falling or staying asleep

(2) irritability or outbursts of anger

(3) difficulty concentrating

(4) hypervigilance

(5) exaggerated startle response

E) Duration of the disturbance is more than one month

F) Causes clinically significant distress or impairment

PYROMANIA

Diagnostic Criteria

A) Deliberate and purposeful fire-setting on more than one occasion

B) Tension or affective arousal before the act

C) Fascination with, interest in, curiosity about, or attraction to fire and its situational contexts

D) Pleasure, gratification, or relief when setting fires, or when witnessing or participating in the aftermath

E) Not done for monetary gain, as an expression of sociopolitical ideology, to conceal criminal activity, express anger or vengeance, improve one's living circumstances, in response to a delusion or hallucination, or as a result of impaired judgment

F) Not better accounted for by conduct disorder, a manic episode, or antisocial personality disorder

Possible Skills

Following Instructions
Accepting "No" Answers
Accepting Criticism
Completing Tasks
Contributing to Discussions
Getting Another Person's Attention
Listening to Others
Making a Request
Participating in Activities
Seeking Positive Attention
Staying on Task
Dealing with Frustration
Delaying Gratification
Relaxation Strategies
Self-Correcting Own Behaviors
Self-Talk or Instruction
Conversation Skills
Greeting Skills
Use of Leisure Time

SCHIZOAFFECTIVE DISORDER

Diagnostic Criteria

A) An uninterrupted period of illness during which at some time there is either a major depressive episode, a manic episode, or a mixed episode concurrent with symptoms that meet Criterion A for schizophrenia

B) During the same period of illness, there have been delusions or hallucinations for at least two weeks in the absence of prominent mood symptoms

C) Symptoms that meet criteria for mood episodes are present for a substantial portion of the total duration of the active and residual periods of the illness

D) The disturbance is not due to the direct physiological effects of a substance or a general medical condition

Specify type:

Bipolar type: if the disturbance includes a manic or a mixed episode (or a manic or a mixed episode and a major depressive episode)

Depressive type: if the disturbance only includes major depressive episodes

Possible Skills

Interacting with Others
Greeting and Departure Skills
Participating in Activities
Positive Statements
Accepting Compliments
Expressing Feelings Appropriately
Optimism
Goal-Setting
Managing Stress
Relaxation
Requesting Help
Assertiveness

SCHIZOPHRENIA

Diagnostic Criteria

A) Characteristic symptoms: Two (or more) of the following, each present for a significant portion of time during a one-month period (or less if successfully treated):

    (1) delusions

    (2) hallucinations

    (3) disorganized speech

    (4) grossly disorganized or catatonic behavior

    (5) negative symptoms

B) Social/occupational dysfunction: For a significant portion of the time since the onset of the disturbance, one or more major areas of functioning are markedly below the level achieved prior to the onset

C) Duration: Continuous signs of disturbance persist for at least six months. This six-month period must include at least one month of symptoms (or less if successfully treated) that meet Criterion A and may include periods of prodromal or residual symptoms. During these prodromal or residual periods, the signs of the disturbances may be manifested by only negative symptoms or two or more symptoms listed in Criterion A present in an attenuated form

D) Schizoaffective and mood disorder exclusion: Schizoaffective disorder and mood disorder with psychotic feature have been ruled out because either (1) no major depressive, manic, or mixed episodes have occurred concurrently with the active-phase symptoms; or (2) if mood episodes have occurred during active-phase symptoms, their total duration has been brief relative to the duration of the active and residual periods

(Continued on next page)

Possible Skills

Greeting and Departure Skills

Conversation Skills

Interrupting Appropriately

Interacting with Others

Assertiveness

Participating in Activities

Structured Problem-Solving

Relaxation

Accepting Criticism

Completing Tasks

Appropriate Appearance

Appropriate Hygiene

Good Quality of Work

Interviewing Skills

Making a Telephone Call

Working Independently

Time Management

Budgeting and Money Management

Job-Finding Strategies

Seeking Professional Assistance

SCHIZOPHRENIA (CONT.)

Diagnostic Criteria

(Continued from previous page)

E) Substance/general medical conditions exclusion: The disturbance is not due to the direct physiological effects of a substance or a general medical condition

F) Relationship to a pervasive development developmental disorder: If there is a history of autistic disorder or another pervasive developmental disorder, the additional diagnosis of schizophrenia is made only if prominent delusions or hallucinations are also present for at least one month

SCHIZOPHRENIFORM DISORDER

Diagnostic Criteria

A) Criteria A, D, and E of schizophrenia are met

B) An episode lasts at least one month but less than six months

Specify:

Without good prognostic feature

With good prognostic feature (as evidenced by two or more of the following):

    (1) onset of prominent psychotic symptoms within four weeks of the first noticeable change in usual behavior or functioning

    (2) confusion or perplexity at the height of psychotic episode

    (3) good premorbid social and occupational functioning

    (4) absence of blunted or flat affect

Possible Skills

Participating in Activities

Accepting Compliments

Expressing Feelings Appropriately

Optimism

Goal-Setting

Managing Stress

Relaxation

Requesting Help

Assertiveness

Expressing Opinions

Accepting Self

Appropriate Appearance

Positive Self-Statements

Coping with Depression

Decision-Making

Rewarding Yourself

Laughing at Oneself

Assessing Own Abilities

SOCIAL PHOBIA

Diagnostic Criteria

A) A marked and persistent fear of one or more social or performance situations in which the person is exposed to unfamiliar people or to possible scrutiny by others. The individual fears that he or she will act in a way that will be humiliating or embarrassing (In children, there must be evidence of the capacity for age-appropriate social relationships with familiar people and the anxiety must occur in peer settings, not just in interactions with adults)

B) Exposure to the feared social situation almost invariably provokes anxiety, which may take the form of a situationally bound or situationally predisposed panic attack (In children, the anxiety may be expressed by crying, tantrums, freezing, or shrinking from social situations with unfamiliar people)

C) The person recognizes that the fear is excessive or unreasonable (In children, this feature may be absent)

D) The feared social or performance situations are avoided or else are endured with intense anxiety or distress

E) The avoidance, anxious anticipation, or distress in the feared social or performance situation(s) interferes significantly with the person's normal routine, occupational (academic) functioning, or social activities or relationships, or there is marked distress about having the phobia

F) In individuals under 18 years, the duration is at least six months

(Continued on next page)

Possible Skills

Interacting with Others
Relaxation Techniques
Identifying Emotions
Asking for Help
Expressing Emotions
Participating in Activities
Time Management
Structured Problem-Solving
Self-Talk or Instruction
Self-Monitoring and Reflection
Seeking Professional Assistance
Dealing with Fear
Conversation Skills
Greeting and Departure Skills
Assertiveness
Goal-Setting
Positive Statements
Controlling Emotions
Preparing for Stressful Events

SOCIAL PHOBIA (CONT.)

Diagnostic Criteria

(Continued from previous page)

G) The fear or avoidance is not due to the direct physiological effects of a substance or a general medical condition and is not better accounted for by another mental disorder

H) If a general medical condition or another mental disorder is present, the fear in Criterion A is unrelated to it

SOMATIZATION DISORDER

Diagnostic Criteria

A) A history of many physical complaints beginning before age 30 years that occur over a period of several years and result in treatment being sought or significant impairment in important areas of functioning

B) Each of the following criteria must have been met, with individual symptoms occurring at any time during the course of the disturbance:

   (1) four pain symptoms: a history of pain related to at least four different steps or functions

   (2) two gastrointestinal symptoms: a history of a least two gastrointestinal symptoms other than pain

   (3) one sexual symptom: a history of at least one sexual or reproductive symptom other than pain

   (4) one pseudoneurological symptom: a history of at least one symptom or deficit suggesting a neurological condition not limited to pain

C) Either (1) or (2):

   (1) after appropriate investigation, each of the symptoms in Criterion B cannot be fully explained by a known medical condition or the direct effects of a substance

   (2) when there is a related general medical condition, the physical complaints or resulting social or occupational impairment are in excess of what would be expected from history, physical examination, or laboratory findings

D) The symptoms are not intentionally produced or feigned

Possible Skills

Engaging in Conversation
Participating in Activities
Positive Self-Statements
Seeking Positive Attention
Coping with Sad Feelings
Expressing Optimism
Stress Management
Laughing at Oneself
Making an Appropriate Complaint
Relaxation
Self-Correcting Own Behavior
Self-Monitoring and Reflection

TRICHOTILLOMANIA

Diagnostic Criteria

A) Recurrent pulling out of one's hair resulting in noticeable hair loss

B) An increasing sense of tension immediately before or when attempting to resist the behavior

C) Pleasure, gratification, or relief when pulling out the hair

D) Not better accounted for by another mental disorder and not due to a general medical condition

E) The disturbance causes clinically significant distress or impairment in important areas of functioning

Possible Skills

Relaxation

Dealing with Frustration

Self-Correcting Own Behaviors

Self-Talk or Instruction

Displaying Appropriate Control

Thought-Stopping

Axis II Disorders

Personality Disorders
and
Mental Retardation

ANTISOCIAL PERSONALITY DISORDER

Diagnostic Criteria

A) A pervasive pattern of disregard for and violation of the rights of others occurring since age 15, as indicated by three (or more) of the following:

(1) failure to conform to social norms with respect to lawful behaviors as indicated by repeatedly performing acts that are grounds for arrest

(2) deceitfulness, as indicated by repeated lying, use of aliases, or conning others for personal profit or pleasure

(3) impulsivity or failure to plan ahead

(4) irritability and aggressiveness, as indicated by repeated physical fights or assaults

(5) reckless disregard for safety of self or others

(6) consistent irresponsibility, as indicated by repeated failure to sustain consistent work behavior or honor financial obligations

(7) lack of remorse, as indicated by being indifferent to or rationalizing having hurt, mistreated, or stolen from another

(B) The individual is at least 18 years of age; there is evidence of conduct disorder with onset before age 15

(C) The occurrence of antisocial behavior is not exclusively during the course of schizophrenia or a manic episode

Possible Skills

Thought-Stopping

Accepting "No" Answers

Disagreeing Appropriately

Accepting Consequences

Accepting Decisions of Authority

Anger Control Strategies

Being on Time

Complying with Reasonable Requests

Following the Rules

Listening to Others

Making an Apology

Seeking Positive Attention

Structured Problem-Solving

Spontaneous Problem-Solving

Saying "No" to Peers

Controlling the Impulse to Lie

Dealing with an Accusation

Following Through on Agreements and Contracts

Keeping Property in Its Place

Problem-Solving a Disagreement

Self-Reporting Own Behavior

AVOIDANT PERSONALITY DISORDER

Diagnostic Criteria

A) A pervasive pattern of social discomfort, fear of negative evaluation, and timidity, beginning by early adulthood and present in a variety of contexts, as indicated by at least four of the following:

(1) avoids occupational activities that involve significant interpersonal contact, because of fears of criticism, disapproval, or rejection

(2) is unwilling to get involved with people unless certain of being liked

(3) shows restraint within intimate relationships because of the fear of being shamed or ridiculed

(4) is preoccupied with being criticized or rejected in social situations

(5) is inhibited in new interpersonal situations because of feelings of inadequacy

(6) views self as socially inept, personally unappealing, or inferior to others

(7) is unusually reluctant to take personal risks or to engage in any new activities because they may prove embarrassing

Possible Skills

Greeting and Departure Skills
Conversation Skills
Assertiveness
Making New Friends
Interacting with Others
Accepting Self
Accepting Compliments
Participating in Activities
Relaxation

BORDERLINE PERSONALITY DISORDER

Diagnostic Criteria

A) A pervasive pattern of instability of inter-personal relationships, self-image and affects, and marked impulsivity beginning by early adulthood and present in a variety of contexts, as indicated by five (or more) of the following:

(1) frantic efforts to avoid real or imagined abandonment

(2) a pattern of unstable and intense interpersonal relationships character-ized by alternating between extremes of idealization and devaluation

(3) identity disturbance: markedly and persistently unstable self-image or sense of self

(4) impulsivity in at least two areas that are potentially self-damaging

(5) recurrent suicidal behavior, gestures, or threats or self-mutilating behavior

(6) affective instability due to a marked reactivity of mood

(7) chronic feelings of emptiness

(8) inappropriate, intense anger or diffi-culty controlling anger

(9) transient, stress-related paranoid ideation or severe dissociative symptoms

Possible Skills

Greeting and Departure Skills
Conversation Skills
Making New Friends
Disagreeing Appropriately
Appropriate Appearance
Appropriate Voice Tone
Giving Compliments
Participating in Activities
Positive Statements about Others
Saying "No" Assertively
Accepting "No" Answers
Accepting Criticism
Accepting Consequences
Anger Control
Complying with Reasonable Requests
Spontaneous Problem-Solving

107

DEPENDENT PERSONALITY DISORDER

Diagnostic Criteria

A) A pervasive and excessive need to be taken care of that leads to submissive and clinging behavior and fears of separation, beginning by early adulthood and present in a variety of contexts, as indicated by five (or more) of the following:

(1) difficulty making decisions without an excessive amount of advice and reassurance from others

(2) needs others to assume responsibility for most major areas of his or her life

(3) has difficulty expressing disagreement with others because of fear of loss of support or approval

(4) difficulty initiating projects or doing things on his or her own (because of lack of self-confidence in judgment of abilities rather than a lack of motivation or energy)

(5) goes to excessive lengths to obtain nurturance and support from others, to the point of volunteering to do things that are unpleasant

(6) feels uncomfortable or helpless when alone because of exaggerated fears of being unable to care for himself or herself

(7) urgently seeks another relationship as a source of care and support when a close relationship ends

(8) unrealistically preoccupied with fears of being left to take care of himself or herself

Possible Skills

Assertiveness
Greeting and Departure Skills
Conversation Skills
Disagreeing Appropriately
Accepting Compliments
Appropriate Appearance
Asking for Help
Appropriate Voice Tone
Participating in Activities
Making New Friends
Willingness to Try New Tasks
Coping with Change
Coping with Sad Feelings
Asking for Advice

NARCISSISTIC PERSONALITY DISORDER

Diagnostic Criteria

A) A pervasive pattern of grandiosity (in fantasy or behavior), need for admiration, and lack of empathy, beginning by early adulthood and present in a variety of contexts, as indicated by five (or more) of the following:

(1) a grandiose sense of self-importance

(2) preoccupied with fantasies of unlimited success, power, brilliance, beauty, or ideal love

(3) believes that he or she is special and unique and can only be understood by, or should associate with, other special or high-status people (or institutions)

(4) requires excessive admiration

(5) a sense of entitlement, i.e., unreasonable expectations of especially favorable treatment or automatic compliance with his or her expectations

(6) interpersonally exploitative, i.e., takes advantage of others to achieve his or her own ends

(7) lacks empathy: is unwilling to recognize or identify with the feelings and needs of others

(8) often envious of others and believes that others are envious of him or her

(9) shows arrogant, haughty behaviors or attitudes

Possible Skills

Showing Sensitivity to Others

Listening Skills

Positive Statements about Others

Expressing Feelings Appropriately

Expressing Empathy and Understanding for Others

Giving Compliments

Conversation Skills

Laughing at Oneself

Tolerating Differences

Responding to Teasing

Maintaining Relationships

Compromising with Others

PARANOID PERSONALITY DISORDER

Diagnostic Criteria

A) A pervasive distrust and suspiciousness of others such that their motives are interpreted as malevolent, beginning by early adulthood and present in a variety of contexts, as indicated by four (or more) of the following:

(1) suspects, without sufficient basis, that others are exploiting, harming, or deceiving him or her

(2) is preoccupied with unjustified doubts about the loyalty or trustworthiness of friends or associates

(3) is reluctant to confide in others because of unwarranted fear that the information will be used maliciously against him or her

(4) reads hidden demeaning or threatening meanings into benign remarks or events

(5) persistently bears grudges, i.e., is unforgiving of insults, injuries, or slights

(6) perceives attacks on character or reputation that are not apparent to others, and is quick to react angrily or to counterattack

(7) has recurrent suspicions, without justification, regarding fidelity of spouse or sexual partner

Possible Skills

Greeting and Departure Skills

Conversation Skills

Participating in Activities

Accepting Help

Acknowledging Others' Presence or Greeting

Positive Statements about Others

Showing Sensitivity to Others

Disagreeing Appropriately

PERSONALITY DISORDER

Diagnostic Criteria

A) A pervasive pattern of excessive emotionality and attention-seeking, beginning by early adulthood and present in a variety of contexts, as indicated by five (or more) of the following:

(1) uncomfortable in situations in which he or she is not the center of attention

(2) interaction with others is often characterized by inappropriate sexually seductive or provocative behavior

(3) displays rapidly shifting and shallow expression of emotions

(4) consistently uses physical appearance to draw attention to self

(5) has a style of speech that is excessively impressionistic and lacking in detail

(6) shows self-dramatization, theatricality, and exaggerated expression of emotion

(7) is suggestible, i.e., easily influenced by others or circumstances

(8) considers relationships to be more intimate than they actually are

Possible Skills

Conversation Skills

Appropriate Voice Tone

Making New Friends

Listening Skills

Greeting and Departure Skills

Interrupting Appropriately

Analyzing Skills Needed
    for Different Situations

Controlling Emotions

Self-Correcting Own Behavior

Self-Monitoring and Reflection

SCHIZOTYPAL PERSONALITY DISORDER

Diagnostic Criteria

A) A pervasive pattern of social and inter-personal deficits marked by acute discomfort with, and reduced capacity for, close relationships as well as by cognitive or perceptual distortions and eccentricities of behavior, beginning by early adulthood and present in a variety of contexts, as indicated by five (or more) of the following:

(1) ideas of reference

(2) odd beliefs or magical thinking that influences behavior and is inconsistent with subcultural norms

(3) unusual perceptual experiences, including bodily illusions

(4) odd thinking and speech

(5) suspiciousness or paranoid ideation

(6) inappropriate or constricted affect

(7) behavior or appearance that is odd, eccentric, or peculiar

(8) lack of close friends or confidants other than first-degree relatives

(9) excessive social anxiety that does not diminish with familiarity and tends to be associated with paranoid fears rather than negative judgments about self

B) Does not occur exclusively during the course of schizophrenia, a mood disorder with psychotic features, another psychotic disorder, or a pervasive developmental disorder

Possible Skills

Greeting and Departure Skills
Conversation Skills
Interacting with Others
Participating in Activities
Acknowledging Others' Presence or Greeting
Appropriate Appearance
Appropriate Voice Tone
Asking for Help
Completing Tasks
Giving Compliments
Personal Hygiene
Positive Statements about Others
Seeking Positive Attention
Willingness to Try New Tasks
Accepting Help or Assistance
Analyzing Skills Needed for Different Situations
Coping with Change
Dealing with Rejection
Making New Friends
Spontaneous Problem-Solving

Chapter 5

Treatment Planning

Treatment planning should be an integral component of the care system in any setting where troubled youth receive care. All members of a treatment team should work together in order to design Treatment Plans that most effectively meet the individual needs of each youth. When Treatment Plans are well-thought out and comprehensive, it is more likely that youth will experience success during treatment, overcome their problems, and lead more happy, fulfilling lives.

This chapter provides three realistic examples (based on the three scenarios at the beginning of the book) of how the information in the charts presented in Chapter 4 can be applied to determine appropriate social skills for children diagnosed with a specific mental health disorder. It also illustrates how to incorporate these skills into an Individual Education Plan (IEP) and Treatment Plans for a group home and a mental health facility. The forms presented here were taken from the Boys Town Wegner Middle School setting, the Boys Town residential group home setting, and the Boys Town psychiatric setting (i.e., Residential Treatment Center). The social skills prescribed as part of the Treatment Plan are in italicized type.

At the end of the chapter is a form labeled "Sample Treatment Plan." This can be used as a guide by caregivers from different treatment settings when they are evaluating and deciding what kind of treatment is most appropriate and therapeutic for youth. Once the initial background information is obtained and filled in, a Treatment Plan can be created based on the facts and data that have been gathered.

The treatment planning process helps to ensure that youth are receiving attention that is focused on their problems. By incorporating Treatment Plans like those presented here, caregivers can increase the likelihood that effective, therapeutic treatment will take place and youth will get better.

Example 1 – 'Slow Learner' Kevin

Synopsis: Kevin is an 11-year-old boy who has been evaluated and diagnosed with Attention-Deficit/ Hyper-activity Disorder by a qualified mental health professional. Symptoms, present since age five, are resulting in significant problems at school and at home. The diagnosis is based on the following *DSM-IV* diagnostic criteria that Kevin is demonstrating both at home and school:

- Difficulty paying or sustaining attention.
- Failure to follow through with instructions.
- Inability to concentrate on details, resulting in careless mistakes.
- Doesn't listen when spoken to directly.
- Easily distracted.
- Regularly loses homework and textbooks.
- Avoids and dislikes completing homework or chores at home.
- Constantly interrupts others and blurts out answers before questions have been completed.
- Doesn't wait his turn.
- Often fidgets with hands and feet, and squirms in his chair.
- Doesn't remain seated in the classroom when required.
- Often is "on the go" or acts as if "driven by a motor."
- Often has difficulty playing or engaging in leisure activities quietly.

BOYS TOWN WEGNER SCHOOL PROGRESS CONFERENCE REPORT
Summary of Social Skills From All Teachers

Student: Kevin Smith   **Grade:** 5th
Core Teacher: Mrs. Jones   **Date:** 2/1/98

SOCIAL SKILLS SUMMARY – From All Subject Areas

Motivation System: Daily ____   Progress __X__   Merit ____

Key:

1 = Frequent Problem   2 = Occasional Problem   3 = Excellent Relations/Behavior

Adult Relations: 1   School Rules: 1

Peer Relations: 1   Classroom Behaviors: 1

Social Skill Areas of Strength: *Greeting Others* and *Appropriate Voice Tone*

Social Skill Areas in Need of Improvement: *Following Instructions, Getting the Teacher's Attention, Seeking Positive Attention, Staying on Task, Completing Tasks*

Number of Office Referrals to Date: 8

Special program modifications or interventions implemented this past year (e.g., behavioral contracts, conferences with Family Teachers, contract for and/or placement in Achievement Plus classroom, etc.):

1. Kevin earns bonus points in the classroom for each 10-minute interval that he **stays on task**. He can use the points on a daily basis at the school store.

2. For **completing tasks on time** (e.g., a classroom task or homework assignment), Kevin earns bonus points that can be used each day at the school store.

3. When Kevin goes one week without an office referral, he earns bonus points for the school auction.

Student enjoys spending his/her points on: Food items, candy, and stickers

New Target Behaviors: *Following Instructions, Getting the Teacher's Attention, Staying on Task, Completing Assignments*

BOYS TOWN WEGNER SCHOOL
INDIVIDUAL EDUCATION PLAN (IEP)

Student: Kevin Smith   **Grade:** 5th
Core Teacher: Mrs. Jones   **Date:** 2/1/98

SOCIAL SKILLS ASSESSMENT – (Core teachers do not fill in)

Motivation System: Points ___   Progress __X__   Merit ___

Behaviors most often resulting in consequences:
Following instructions, getting teacher's attention, staying on task, completing assignments

Behaviors most often reinforced:
Greeting others, asking for help, being on time, appropriate voice tone

---

CURRICULUM AREAS TO BE COVERED THIS:
TRIMESTER   <u>SEMESTER</u>   YEAR

Introduction to basic concepts in:
*1) Nature of the outdoors   2) Fossils   3) Magnetism, Electricity
4) Oceans   5) Current issues in science*

SOCIAL SKILLS CHECKLIST (Ratings from checklist summary)

1- Frequent Problems
2-Occasional Problems
3-Excellent relations/Behavior

ADULT RELATIONS	1	<u>2</u>	3
PEER RELATIONS	1	<u>2</u>	3
SCHOOL RULES	<u>1</u>	2	3
CLASSROOM BEHAVIORS	<u>1</u>	2	3

OTHER OBSERVATIONS: Kevin has a difficult time concentrating on any task for longer than a few minutes. This leads to negative consequences and frustration for Kevin. I have seen more defiant and acting-out behaviors in my class since the last report.

THIS STUDENT WILL IMPROVE HIS/HER SOCIAL SKILLS BY _____
Adult relations, peer relations, classroom behaviors, following school rules (Indicate one or more areas. If none, write "none at this time" after #1)

THROUGH EMPHASIS ON THE FOLLOWING SOCIAL SKILLS:

Date Started	Date Ended	
2/98		*Following Instructions*
2/98		*Getting Teacher's Attention*
2/98		*Staying on Task*
2/98		*Completing Tasks*

Measurement Devices: Point card review, teacher observations

ADJUSTMENTS IN METHODS, CONTENT, LEVEL, ETC., NECESSARY TO MEET THE INDIVIDUAL NEEDS OF THIS STUDENT

(Tape recorder; oral tests; learning activity packets; seating; precision teaching channels - see/say, think/say, hear/say, hear/touch, hear/write, think/write, etc.; length of assignments; peer tutoring; and so on.) If none, write "none at this time" after #1.

Date Started

2/98	*Kevin earns bonus points in the classroom for each 10-minute interval that he stays on task. He can use these points at the school store.*
2/98	*For completing tasks on time, Kevin earns bonus points that can be used each day at the school store.*
2/98	*When Kevin goes one week without an office referral, he earns bonus points for the school auction.*

Rationales for above adjustments determined by: (Observations, formal tests, informal tests, medical reports, etc.) Point card review and teacher observations.

123

Example 2 – 'Unmanageable' Dwayne

Synopsis: Dwayne is a 12-year-old boy who has been evaluated and diagnosed with Oppositional Defiant Disorder by a qualified mental health professional. Symptoms, present for more than a year, are resulting in significant problems at school, home, and in the community. This diagnosis is based on the following *DSM-IV* diagnostic criteria that Kevin demonstrates at home and school:

- Often loses his temper.
- Regularly argues with adults.
- Often defies or refuses to comply with adults' requests or rules.
- Blames others for his mistakes and misbehavior.
- Deliberately annoys others and is spiteful and vindictive.

TREATMENT PLAN
BOYS TOWN GROUP HOME PROGRAM

Name: Dwayne Jackson   **Motivation System:** Daily   **Date:** 2/1/98

Diagnostic/Referral Problem: Oppositional Defiant Disorder

Target Skill: #1 *Accepting Consequences*

Baseline: Percent of teaching to target skill per week = 14%

   Frequency of problem behavior per week = 16 incidents

   Percent of positive displayed skill per week = 10%

Problem Definition:

When given a consequence, Dwayne complains and makes excuses. He blames others for his behavior. Often, he begins to shout and becomes verbally abusive; this is more prevalent when he is not expecting a consequence (e.g., phone call from school about his negative behavior). These behaviors happen regardless of who gave the consequence or the amount of the consequence.

Long-Term Goal: Percent of teaching to target skill per week = 25%

   Frequency of problem behavior per week = 0-1 incidents

   Percent of positive displayed skill per week = 80%

Treatment Strategies:

Social Skill Teaching: 1) Quiz Dwayne on the components of accepting consequences two times per day; 2) Role-play pretend situation one time per day; 3) Preventively prompt before each consequence; 4) Spontaneously use Teaching Interactions for positive and negative behavior; 5) During Family Meeting, accepting consequences will be taught and reviewed a minimum of one time per week; 6) When Dwayne reduces the frequency of his problem behavior by one-half during any week, he earns a predetermined "special."

Therapy: Dwayne will attend individual therapy with Dr. Smith once a week for one-half hour.

Medications: None at this time.

_____	_____	_____
Youth	**Family-Teacher**	**Consultant**

TREATMENT PLAN
BOYS TOWN GROUP HOME PROGRAM

Name: Dwayne Jackson **Motivation System:** Daily **Date:** 2/1/98

Diagnostic/Referral Problem: Oppositional Defiant Disorder

Target Skill: #2 *Accepting Decisions of Authority*

Baseline: **Percent of teaching to target skill per week** = 11%

Frequency of problem behavior per week = 25 incidents

Percent of positive displayed skill per week = 2%

Problem Definition:

When Dwayne is approached by an authority figure (i.e., parents, Family-Teacher, teachers, youth manager, etc.) regarding a task to be done or a rule he broke or an incident he was involved in, he frequently loses self-control. He begins by arguing; when he realizes he will not get his way, he escalates into shouting and cursing, and often becomes verbally aggressive.

Long-Term Goal: **Percent of teaching to target skill per week** = 25%

Frequency of problem behavior per week = 0-1 incidents

Percent of positive displayed skill per week = 80%

Treatment Strategies:

Social Skill Teaching: 1) Quiz Dwayne on the components of accepting adult authority two times per day; 2) Role-play pretend situation one time per day; 3) Preventively prompt as situation demands; 4) Spontaneously use Teaching Interactions for positive and negative behavior; 5) During Family Meeting, accepting adult authority will be taught and reviewed a minimum of one time per week; 6) When Dwayne reduces the frequency of his problem behavior by one-half during any week, he earns a predetermined "special."

Therapy: Dwayne will attend individual therapy with Dr. Smith once a week for one-half hour.

Medications: None at this time.

Youth	Family-Teacher	Consultant

TREATMENT PLAN
BOYS TOWN GROUP HOME PROGRAM

Name: Dwayne Jackson   **Motivation System:** Daily   **Date:** 2/1/98

Diagnostic/Referral Problem: Oppositional Defiant Disorder

Target Skill: #3 *Expressing Feelings Appropriately*

Baseline: **Percent of teaching to target skill per week** = 9%

               Frequency of problem behavior per week = 21 incidents

               Percent of positive displayed skill per week = 8%

Problem Definition:

When confronted with situations that frustrate or upset him, Dwayne often loses self-control. He expresses how he feels by arguing and yelling. Frequently, he escalates his behavior to cursing and often becomes verbally abusive and verbally aggressive. Occasionally, he causes property damage by throwing things, although not at people.

Long-Term Goal: **Percent of teaching to target skill per week** = 25%

               Frequency of problem behavior per week = 0-1 incidents

               Percent of positive displayed skill per week = 80%

Treatment Strategies:

Social Skill Teaching: 1) Quiz Dwayne on the components of expressing feelings appropriately two times per day; 2) Role-play pretend situation one time per day; 3) Preventively prompt as situation demands; 4) Spontaneously use Teaching Interactions for positive and negative behavior; 5) During Family Meeting, expressing feelings appropriately will be taught and reviewed a minimum of one time per week; 6) Dwayne will keep a "feelings log" and share it with his Family-Teachers (and therapist) each night.

Therapy: Dwayne will attend individual therapy with Dr. Smith once a week for one-half hour.

Medications: None at this time.

_____	_____	_____
Youth	**Family-Teacher**	**Consultant**

Example 3 – 'Down in the Dumps' Jamie

Synopsis: Jamie is a 13-year-old girl who has been evaluated and diagnosed with Major Depressive Disorder, Recurrent by a qualified mental health professional. Symptoms are resulting in significant problems at school, at home, and with friends. This diagnosis is based on the following *DSM-IV* diagnostic criteria that Jamie is demonstrating at home and school:

- Two suicide attempts in the last 12 months.
- Depressed mood most of the day, most every day, as reported and observed by parents and teachers.
- Diminished interest in daily activities and previously pleasurable activities.
- Significant weight loss.
- Insomnia.
- Feelings of worthlessness.
- Diminished ability to think and concentrate.
- Fatigue and loss of energy.

COMPREHENSIVE TREATMENT PLAN
BOYS TOWN RESIDENTIAL TREATMENT CENTER

Date of Admission: January 1, 1998

Name: Jamie Jones   **Date of Initial Treatment Plan:** January 10, 1998

Medical Record Number: 00-00-00

Priority		Problem List
Yes	No	
X		History of self-harm statements and attempts.
X		Acts out aggressively (including assault).
X		Difficulty expressing feelings appropriately.
X		Symptoms of depression (e.g., withdrawn, tearful, easily distracted, low self-esteem).
X		Poor coping skills.
X		Family relationship issues.
X		Poor anger/impulse control.
X		Difficulty accepting decisions of authority.
X		Behind on school credits.
X		History of drug and alcohol use.
	X	Sexual molestation – will address if Jamie feels she is ready to discuss.

Each "No" response requires a rationalization to be listed following the problem.

Strengths: Motivated to change, intelligent, able to care about others, and has good social skills.

COMPREHENSIVE TREATMENT PLAN

Name: Jamie Jones   **DOB:** 6/14/85   **MR #:** 00-00-00

Date of Admission: January 1, 1998

Medication: Zoloft (50 mg.) in the morning.

Goal: Jamie will decrease symptoms of depression (e.g., withdrawn, tearful, easily distracted, low self-esteem, and others) while increasing her ability to *express feelings appropriately*.

Objective #1: Jamie will increase her ability to *express her feelings appropriately* to a rate of 90% as measured across all areas by February 15, 1998.

_____ **Date Achieved**

Objective #2: Jamie will increase her ability to *express feelings appropriately* regarding family issues in individual, family, and group therapy to a rate of 90% as measured across all areas by February 15, 1998.

_____ **Date Achieved**

Objective #3: Jamie will increase her ability to *use positive self-statements* to a rate of 90% as measured across all areas by February 15, 1998.

_____ **Date Achieved**

Objective #4: Jamie will increase her ability to *participate in activities* to a rate of 90% as measured across all areas by February 15, 1998.

_____ **Date Achieved**

Objective #5: Jamie will participate in drug and alcohol education group two times a month and discuss her past drug and alcohol use.

_____ **Date Achieved**

Persons Responsible: Doug Smith, MD; Dawn Johnson, MSW; Rick Doe,
Unit Coordinator

*See the Boys Town manual, *Teaching Social Skills to Youth*,
for the steps to the skills listed above.

Jamie Jones
DOB: 6/17/85
MR #: 00-00-00

Goal: Jamie will decrease her aggression while increasing her ability to *accept decisions of those in authority**.

Objective #1: Jamie will increase her ability to *accept decisions of authority** to the rate of 90% as measured across all areas by February 15, 1998.

_____ **Date Achieved**

Objective #2: Jamie will reduce the number of aggressive incidents (i.e., assaults) to "0" for 30 days by February 15, 1998.

_____ **Date Achieved**

Objective #3: Jamie will increase her ability to *control emotions** and deal with frustration and anger to a rate of 90% by *using her self-control strategies** of deep-breathing and visual imagery by February 15, 1998.

_____ **Date Achieved**

Persons Responsible: Doug Smith, MD; Dawn Johnson, MSW; Rick Doe, Unit Coordinator

*See the Boys Town manual, *Teaching Social Skills to Youth*, for the steps to the skills listed above.

131

Jamie Jones
DOB: 6/17/85
MR #: 00-00-00

Goal: Jamie will improve confidence in her academic abilities and *study skills**.

Objective #1: Jamie will remain on task when directed as demonstrated by *accepting help or assistance**, *asking for help**, and *participating in activities** in the classroom four out of seven class periods by February 15, 1998.

_____ **Date Achieved**

Objective #2: Jamie will *complete tasks** (i.e., school assignments) at 80% accuracy in five out of seven class periods by February 15, 1998.

_____ **Date Achieved**

Objective #3: Jamie will *spontaneously problem-solve** with peers and staff when conflicts arise in the classroom four out of seven class periods by February 19, 1998.

_____ **Date Achieved**

Objective #4: Jamie will attempt to *be more assertive** and *resist peer pressure** four out of seven class periods by February 19, 1998.

_____ **Date Achieved**

Persons Responsible: Cathy Wilson, MA

*See the Boys Town manual, Teaching Social Skills to Youth,
for the steps to the skills listed above.

Jamie Jones
DOB: 6/17/85
MR #: 00-00-00

COMPREHENSIVE TREATMENT PLAN REVIEW

Treatment Strategies: Individual, group, and family therapy that incorporates cognitive-behavioral strategies, family system strategies, a therapeutic milieu, cognitive-behavioral concepts, medications, and a level system that uses cognitive-behavioral concepts.

Data Collection: Weekly medical chart probes, professional observation, and motivational system card data.

Treatment Team Reviews

Review 1: Date: February 17, 1998

During this review period, Jamie has made minimal progress on all objectives. She has engaged in nine incidents of physical aggression and has been physically assaultive toward peers and staff on four occasions. Jamie also has made five self-harm statements and engaged in two incidents of self-destructive behavior. Due to these statements and behaviors, Dr. Smith placed Jamie on suicide evaluation on three separate occasions; therefore, a new objective will be designed so that the occurrences of these statements and behaviors can continue to be measured.

Review 2: Date: _____

Review 3: Date: _____

Review 4: Date: _____

Jamie Jones
DOB: 6/17/85
M R #: 00-00-00

DISCHARGE PLAN

Estimated length of stay: Three to four months.

Criteria For Discharge: No incidents of aggression for 30 days.

Projected Placement: Group living environment.

Transition: 15-30 days.

Psychiatric Consultation: Ongoing for monitoring of medications and mental health needs.

Therapy: Individual and group sessions with unit therapist.

Medical: None.

Other: Parents will attend and complete a Boys Town Common Sense Parenting® course.

Treatment Team Reviews

Review 1: Date: February 17, 1998

Review of Discharge Plan and Reason for Continued Care:

During this review period, Jamie has had several behavioral difficulties within the classroom setting; this environment seems to be her greatest source of frustration. Jamie also has had difficulty controlling her anger impulses and has made several self-harm statements instead of expressing her feelings appropriately. Continued practice, effort, and improvement is needed before Jamie will be able to move to a less-restrictive level of care.

Jamie's parents are enrolled in and will attend a Boys Town Common Sense Parenting course next month.

Review 2: Date: _____

Review of Discharge Plan and Reason for Continued Care:

Review 3: Date: _____

Review of Discharge Plan and Reason for Continued Care:

SAMPLE TREATMENT PLAN

Youth: _____ Treatment Team: _____

Leader _____

Date of Birth _____/ _____/ _____ Date of Admission _____/ _____/ _____

Review Period _____/ _____/ _____ to _____/ _____/ _____

I. Projected length of stay and discharge criteria

II. Problem/Needs

	Date Identified	Date Revised	Date Achieved
Problem #1			
Goals			
Treatment Objectives and Timelines			
Treatment Services, Frequencies and Responsible Parties			

	Date Identified	Date Revised	Date Achieved
Problem #2			
Goals			
Treatment Objectives and Timelines			
Treatment Services, Frequencies and Responsible Parties			

	Date Identified	Date Revised	Date Achieved
Problem #3			
Goals			
Treatment Objectives and Timelines			
Treatment Services, Frequencies and Responsible Parties			

Youth _____   Date _____

Parent _____   Date _____

Family Teacher/Treatment Parent/Youth Care Worker _____   Date _____

Referring Agency _____   Date _____

TREATMENT PLANNING WORKSHEET

Youth Name: Date:

Problem Identification (Functional Analysis):

Alternative Replacement/Social Skills	Contingent Consequences	
	+	**–**
1.		
2.		
3.		
4.		
5.		
6.		

Cognitive Strategy:	Feeling Strategy:
Corrective Teaching Strategy:	Praising Strategy:
Relationship Development Strategy:	Self-Government Strategy:
Medication Regime:	Individual /Group Therapy:

Generalization Strategy (School, Home/Program, Work, Other)

Appendix

The Boys Town Continuum of Care

Quality child care is something the American public has a right to demand. But many people have given up on today's children and families. Boys Town has not. Boys Town's philosophy of care combines state-of-the-art, technology-based services to meet the needs of troubled youth and families. All of our technologies are research proven and outcome oriented. They can and do change the behaviors and attitudes of children and families in crisis.

So far in this book we have discussed how social skill instruction plays a vital role in the treatment of children and adolescents with mental health disorders. We also have illustrated how teaching social skills can help youth improve their lives in a variety of child-care settings. This chapter will focus on the specific Boys Town programs that incorporate social skill instruction and other components of treatment, and explain how they are connected in Boys Town's Continuum of Care. Given this context, it will be easy to see why Boys Town carries out its mission the way it does.

Each program in Boys Town's Continuum of Care focuses on three essential goals that are the core of the Boys Town Teaching Model: Building relationships, teaching skills, and empowering children through teaching self-control. These three qualities are the hallmarks of healing and hope. Boys Town's services address a wide array of treatment issues, from prevention to remediation, from dealing with behavioral problems to treating mental health disorders. And all of the programs have the basic tenets that have proven effective in Boys Town's residential programs.

Boys Town committed itself to creating a continuum of care in 1988 after evaluating the effectiveness of and consumer satisfaction with its treatment technology. As a result, Boys Town developed new programs that adapted and restructured this technology to meet the specific and individual needs of their clients.

The consistency of treatment across our continuum enables youth and their families to reap the maximum benefits from whatever treatment they receive. This consistency also makes it less likely that the learned skills will deteriorate as youth move to less-restrictive points on the continuum.

The goal of each program is to provide the best quality care. To accomplish this, five essential components must be in place:

1. **The program and its environment must be safe.** Policies and procedures must be in place and adhered to at all times.

2. **The children must be happy in the program.** Our staff members – either through direct care for youth or families, or through training and consultation – are mandated to create and maintain a healthy, emotionally enriching atmosphere for each and every youth.

3. **The children must get better.** Boys Town believes in outcomes, not rhetoric.

4. **Programs must be family oriented and family based.** Staff members must create and promote family skills and family values in order for children to learn responsible behavior.

5. **Programs must be replicable.** Each program must be designed so that it can be taught to and used by other child-care organizations and services. Only then can Boys Town truly carry out its mission of "changing the way America cares for her at-risk children and families."

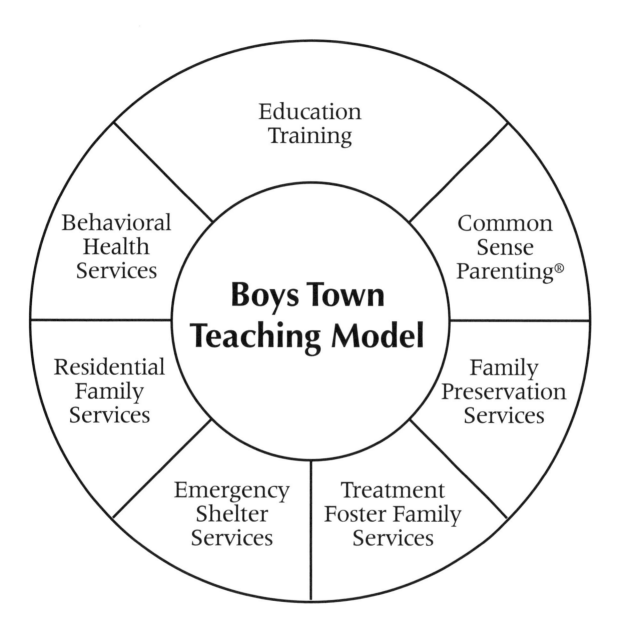

Education Training

Common Sense Parenting®

Behavioral Health Services

Boys Town Teaching Model

Family Preservation Services

Residential Family Services

Emergency Shelter Services

Treatment Foster Family Services

Programs in the Continuum of Care

Education Training

For the past 25 years, educators who completed the Phi Delta Kappan/Gallup poll identified discipline as one of the biggest problems in American schools. For 17 of those 25 years, educators considered it the number one problem. The Boys Town Education Model trains teachers in how to teach social skills to students and how to make this teaching part of the regular school curriculum. Educators learn a systematic approach for addressing appropriate and inappropriate behaviors, and are provided with a definition of when students should be referred to the office and procedures for doing this. This training enables educators to focus on teaching academics, rather than controlling behavior, as students learn how to better manage their own behavior.

Distinctive Characteristics:

- Social Skill Curriculum – This set of 16 basic social skills for youth encompasses relationships with adults and peers, school rules, and classroom behaviors.

- Teaching Interactions® – These techniques combine efforts to manage student behavior by teaching alternative appropriate behaviors and providing praise for prosocial behavior.

- Motivation Systems – This three-level token economy is designed so that special education programs can meet each student's individual needs while providing a gradual transition from artificial consequences to more naturally occurring forms of feedback and internal controls.

- Administrative Intervention® – This is an established sequence of teaching methods that are used with youth who are referred to the office for inappropriate or disruptive behavior, or loss of self-control. The process, which includes teaching alternative behaviors that promote consistency and predictability, has as its goal the successful return of the student to the classroom.

Common Sense Parenting

Boys Town's Common Sense Parenting® is for parents who want to become better parents and learn new ways to deal with their children's problem behaviors. Common Sense Parenting has taken Boys Town's proven child-care methods for troubled children and adapted them to meet the needs of single- and two-parent families. The program offers a six-session class schedule that allows parents to learn, practice, and demonstrate new parenting skills. Program components involve instruction, videotape modeling, role-playing, feedback, and review.

Distinctive Characteristics:

- The Common Sense Parenting program is a cost-effective, short-term (6 weeks, 12 hours) group intervention that is designed to increase parental competence and improve child behavior.

- A hallmark of the skill-oriented, competency-based program is having parents practice skills (i.e., role-play).

- Professionals teach skills and provide instruction, consultation, and support.

- Parents are taught positive alternatives to physical punishment.

- The Common Sense Parenting program can be used alone or as a component of a more-intensive family treatment program.

Family Preservation Services/In-Home Crisis Intervention

Boys Town's Family Preservation Services provides intensive in-home treatment for families in crisis. This unique program helps parents build on their strengths and develop individual parenting skills. Family Preservation Services helps heal family pain and abuse through support, problem-solving, and therapy.

Distinctive Characteristics:

- Crisis stabilization services are delivered in the home with a focus on the whole family.

- Intensive short-term services are delivered within a six- to eight-week time frame.

- Interventions and treatment focus on teaching cognitive and behavioral skills that are needed for family preservation or reunification.

- Interventions are community-based with a goal of linking families to needed services and teaching skills for accessing services.

- Treatment professionals are on call 24 hours a day, 7 days a week.

- Treatment is individualized to take advantage of each family's strengths and agendas.

- Less-intensive Family Preservation programs and early crisis intervention services also are available.

Treatment Foster Family Services

Boys Town's Treatment Foster Family Services provides an out-of-home placement option for children and adolescents who, for one reason or another, are unable to live at home, and whose special needs hinder their success in a traditional foster care placement. Boys Town Treatment Foster Parents receive the training and support services necessary to provide a healing and nurturing home environment for these children, helping them overcome their problems and live normal, productive lives.

Distinctive Characteristics:

- Family homes in the community serve as the treatment setting for children ages 2 to 18 years.

- One child is placed in each Treatment Foster Home.

- This is an intermediate program for children who cannot live with their own families or with traditional foster families.

- The program provides an alternative to placement in more-restrictive settings.

- Treatment Foster Parents are trained in Boys Town treatment technology and are the primary treatment agents. They receive weekly consultation and supervision, and emergency backup (24 hours a day, 7 days a week) from professionals on staff.

- Individual Treatment Plans focus on specific youth behaviors.

- Treatment Foster Parents and professional staff participate in an annual skill-based certification process that is based on performance and consumer satisfaction ratings.

Emergency Shelter Services/Crisis Stabilization

Boys Town's Emergency Shelter Services provides a needed safety net for children and families in crisis. This emergency care intervention program helps abused, neglected, runaway, and troubled youth ages 10 to 18, and offers individual treatment planning to help youth deal with their problems. The program also strives to reunify and strengthen families by offering mediation and counseling.

Distinctive Characteristics:

- Youth are treated in a family-style environment.

- Individualized Treatment Plans target specific problem behaviors.

- Treatment focuses on teaching needed social and self-control skills.

- Family reunification or movement of a youth to a less-restrictive environment is a primary goal of treatment.

- Youth Care Workers participate in an annual certification process that is based on performance and consumer satisfaction ratings.

Residential Family Services

The goal of Boys Town's Residential Family Services program is to teach troubled youth new and appropriate skills in a family setting. Each home is staffed by a professionally trained married couple called Family-Teachers and a helper called an Assistant Family-Teacher.

The Family-Teachers live in the residential homes with 6 to 8 boys or girls 24 hours a day, providing guidance, teaching social skills to the youth, and meeting their individual needs.

Distinctive Characteristics:

- At-risk children, ages 10 to 18, receive treatment in a family-living environment.

- Family-Teachers are extensively trained in the Boys Town Teaching Model and serve as the primary treatment agents for youth in their homes.

- Professional staff supervise and consult weekly with Family-Teachers regarding development and implementation of Treatment Plans.

- Professional staff are on call 24 hours a day, 7 days a week to provide backup and crisis intervention as needed.

- Family-Teachers participate in an annual certification process that is based on performance and consumer satisfaction ratings.

Behavioral Health Services

Boys Town's Behavioral Health Services provides assistance to inpatient child and adolescent psychiatric hospitals, residential treatment centers/facilities, day treatment programs, and other programs that care for youth with more severe behavior problems and/or mental health disorders. Through Behavioral Health Services, Boys Town offers training and consultation in its Psychoeducational Treatment Model (PEM). The PEM is adapted from the Boys Town Teaching Model and is a multidisciplinary process for child and adolescent treatment that is designed to supplement and support the more traditional forms of treatment. Staff use the techniques from the PEM around the clock to teach patients social skills, reinforce adaptive behaviors, and solve problems.

Distinctive Characteristics:

- The PEM employs a "bio-psycho-social" approach to treatment.

- Social skills teaching serves as an adjunct to the medical model traditionally found in mental health settings.

- Building relationships with troubled children and adolescents is a major component of treatment.

- An easy-to-learn interaction process enables staff members to successfully work with children and adolescents who are in crisis and have lost self-control.

- Kids are taught self-control skills that empower them to de-escalate (and ultimately stop) aggressive, violent, and self-destructive behaviors when they become upset or frustrated.

- Treatment focuses on generalizing learned social skills to other environments (e.g., home, school, and other less-restrictive placements) so that children are set up for success when they leave the treatment facility.

Summary

Boys Town offers youth and their care providers a continuum of therapeutic services, all of which promote three basic goals: building relationships, teaching skills, and empowering children through teaching self-control. The services Boys Town provides within its Continuum of Care include Education Training, Common Sense Parenting, Family Preservation Services/In-Home Crisis Intervention, Treatment Foster Family Services, Emergency Shelter Services/Crisis Stabilization, Residential Family Services, and Behavioral Health Services. With the integration of this delivery system, youth are able to move into a more-restrictive or less-restrictive setting, depending on their progress and treatment needs. Finally, each of these services is grounded in the Boys Town Teaching Model. Because of this basic program compatibility, we believe there is a greater chance for successful treatment of youth and families.

References

Achenbach, T.M. (1991). **Manual for the child behavior checklist/ 4-18 and 1991 profile**. Burlington, VT: University of Vermont Department of Psychiatry.

American Psychiatric Association. (1994). **Diagnostic and statistical manual of mental disorders**. (4th ed.). Washington, DC: American Psychiatric Association.

Combs, M.L., & Slaby, D.A. (1977). Social skills training with children. In B.B. Lahey & A.E. Kazdin (Eds.), **Advances in clinical child psychology** (pp. 161-201). New York: Plenum Press.

Dowd, T., & Tierney, J. (1992). **Teaching social skills to youth: A curriculum for child-care providers**. Boys Town, NE: Boys Town Press.

Friman, P.C. (1997). Behavioral, family-style residential care for troubled out-of-home adolescents: Recent findings. In J.E. Carr and J. Austin (Eds.), **Handbook of applied behavior analysis**. Reno, NV: Context Press.

Gaw, A.C. (Ed.) (1993). **Culture, ethnicity, and mental illness**. Washington, D.C: American Psychiatric Press, Inc.

Glomb, N. (1996). **Do social skills programs accommodate cultural diversity? A review of secondary curricula**. Paper presented at the 74th annual conference of the Council for Exceptional Children, Orlando, FL.

Peter, V.J. (1999). **What makes Boys Town successful**. Boys Town, NE: Boys Town Press.

Thompson, R.W., & Teare, J.F. (1997, June). **Measuring outcomes across a continuum of programs in the managed care environment**. Paper presented at the Professional Child Care Conference, Boys Town, NE.

Index

A

B

D

E

F

G

H

I

K

M

T

U

W